one million things

ANIMAL LIFE

**LONDON, NEW YORK,
MELBOURNE, MUNICH, AND DELHI**

Project editor Jenny Finch
Senior designer Stefan Podhorodecki
Designers Sheila Collins, Katie Knutton, Philip Letsu, Hoa Luc,
Marilou Prokopiou, Smiljka Surla

Commissioned photography Dave King
Creative retouching Steve Willis
Picture research Nic Dean
Production editor Hitesh Patel
Production controller Angela Graef
Jacket design Akiko Kato, Junkichi Tatsuki
Jacket editor Mariza O'Keeffe
Design development manager Sophia M Tampakopoulos Turner
US editor Margaret Parrish

Managing editor Linda Esposito
Managing art editor Diane Thistlethwaite
Publishing manager Andrew Macintyre
Category publisher Laura Buller

First published in the United States in 2009
by DK Publishing
375 Hudson Street
New York, New York 10014

09 10 11 12 13 10 9 8 7 6 5 4 3 2 1
WD208 – 04/09

DK books are available at special discounts when purchased in bulk for
sales promotions, premiums, fundraising, or educational use. For details, contact:
DK Publishing Special Markets
375 Hudson Street
New York, New York 10014
SpecialSales@dk.com

A catalog record for this book is
available from the Library of Congress.

ISBN: 978-0-7566-5234-0

Hi res workflow proofed by AltaImage, UK
Design and digital artworking by Stefan Podhorodecki
Printed and bound by LEO, China

**Discover more at
www.dk.com**

one million things

ANIMAL LIFE

Written by:

Richard Walker

Consultant:

Kim Bryan

1

Diversity

2

Life skills

3

Lifestyles

Contents

SAVANNA WILDLIFE
At a waterhole in the African savanna, giraffes, zebras, birds, and other thirsty animals gather to drink. These creatures are a tiny sample of the enormous variety of animals found worldwide.

Diversity

LIFE

From microscopic bacteria to massive blue whales, planet Earth is populated by a spectacular variety of life. But, despite their obvious differences, all living things share certain common features. They all obtain energy, grow, respond to their surroundings, and reproduce—things that nonliving objects, such as rocks, cannot do. Scientists divide life-forms into five distinct groups called kingdoms. Each has its own features, as you can see here.

Staphylococcus

BACTERIA ▶

These are the tiniest, most abundant, and most widespread life-forms. Bacteria consist of single cells that, despite being simpler than those in other organisms, work in the same basic ways. Some take in food from their surroundings, while others make their own, using sunlight or other sources of energy.

Amoeba

Helicobacter pylori

◀ PROTISTS

Like bacteria, most protists also consist of single cells, but they are larger and just as complex as the cells that form animals and plants. Protists generally live in water or damp places. They are divided into animal-like protozoa, which take in food from their surroundings, and plantlike algae, which make food by photosynthesis.

Fly agaric

Paramecium

Puffballs

Dried yeast

FUNGI ▶

Mushrooms, toadstools, molds, and yeasts are just some of the organisms that make up the fungi. Some resemble plants, but they live in a very different way. Fungi feed by releasing digestive chemicals called enzymes that break down dead or living matter, then absorb the simple nutrients that are released.

Bread mold

Bracket fungus

ANIMALS ▼

Despite their diversity, all animals share certain key features. They are all multicellular (made from many cells), and get their food by eating other living things. All animals move at least part of their body, and many move around actively to find their food, using one or more senses to detect it.

South American tapir

Llama

Koala

Strawberry shrimp

Pheasant

Mudskipper

Porcupine

Mangrove rat snake

Horsefly

Nautilus

Iguana

Rat

Crab

Armadillo

Hissing cockroach

PLANTS ▶

From grasses to giant trees, all plants require water, sunlight, and soil in which to grow their roots. Most plants do not move actively or feed on other organisms. Instead, they use a process called photosynthesis, trapping sunlight energy to turn carbon dioxide and water into food.

Lily

Moss

Grass

Ivy

fixed to that spot as adults. Sponges are the simplest of all animals, with no regular shape. They feed by filtering out food particles from a current of water that they draw in through pores (holes) in their body.

others, including anemones, are anchored to rocks. Many are carnivores that capture prey using their stinging tentacles. Some Cnidaria species are actually colonies of many individual organisms.

Phylum Annelida includes worms with bodies divided into segments, such as earthworms, leeches, and ragworms. Phylum Platyhelminthes includes the flatworms, with their flattened, ribbonlike bodies.

distinct head and body segments, and legs with joints. The main arthropod groups are the insects, the crustaceans, such as crabs and crayfish, and the arachnids, which feature spiders and scorpions.

ANIMAL KINGDOM

The animal kingdom contains an extraordinary variety of different species, which can be arranged into 34 groups called phyla. Just one of these phyla, the Chordata, includes all vertebrates (animals with backbones, such as fish, ferrets, and frogs). The other more than 30 phyla contain 97 percent of known animal species, and are known collectively as invertebrates (animals without backbones), even though they are distantly related and share few common features. Here are some of the animal kingdom's main phyla.

❺ MOLLUSCA

This group of soft-bodied animals includes many that are protected by shells, such as slow-moving snails, whelks, and limpets, as well as bivalves (those with a shell in two hinged halves), such as mussels, that barely move at all. By contrast, the cephalopod branch of the phylum includes mollusks such as squid, cuttlefish, and octopuses that are intelligent and can shoot rapidly through water.

❻ ECHINODERMATA

Unlike other animals, the echinoderms, or "spiny-skinned animals," have a body divided into five parts arranged like the spokes of a wheel around a central point, and a supportive skeleton made of hard plates lying just beneath the skin. The phylum includes starfish, brittlestars, sea urchins, and sea cucumbers, all of which, as some of their names suggest, live in the sea.

❼ CHORDATA

The majority of chordates are vertebrates, which include the largest animals. They have a backbone that forms part of an internal, flexible skeleton that supports the body and is moved by attached muscles. They also have four limbs and a highly developed nervous system and sense organs. Vertebrates include birds, mammals, reptiles, amphibians, and the various types of fish. Chordates that are not vertebrates include sea squirts and lancelets.

7. KINGDOM ▶

At the top of the classification hierarchy is the animal kingdom, which contains more than 30 phyla. The other highly diverse phyla aside from the chordates are usually grouped together as "invertebrates" because they have no backbones, although this term has no meaning in classification. They include arthropods (insects, spiders, and crabs), mollusks, and worms.

6. PHYLUM ▶

Animals are grouped into phyla according to their main features. Mammals and related classes—including fish, birds, reptiles, and amphibians—belong to the phylum Chordata (the chordates). They all have a nerve cord running down their back and, at some stage in their life, a rod of tissue called a notochord. Most chordates are vertebrates—animals whose notochord grows into a backbone.

▶ 5. CLASS

There are 27 diverse orders that make up the class Mammalia (mammals), ranging from carnivores, bats, and seals, to primates (including humans) and kangaroos. Despite their diversity, all mammals are endothermic (warm-blooded), suckle their young with milk, and most have hair. No other class of animals shows these last two features.

Butterfly

Octopus

Crab

Land snail

Tarantula

Dragonfly

Toucan

Crocodile

Angelfish

Python

Frog

Bat

Kangaroo

Sea lion

Parrot

Penguin

Orang-utan

Tiger

Polar bear

CLASSIFICATION

There are 1.5 million known species (types) of animal on Earth, with millions more yet to be discovered. Scientists make sense of this vast array of creatures by looking for similarities and differences between species and organizing them into groups of increasing size—from a genus, which contains related species, through family, order, class, and phylum, to kingdom, which includes all animal species. In this example, you can see which groups the least weasel belongs to, and how it relates to other species.

▲ 4. ORDER

Eight families, including mustelids, cats, bears, dogs, and foxes, make up the order Carnivora. Those belonging to this order share certain features: most eat meat, are the predominant skilled hunters and predators on land, and have flesh-slicing teeth. Some, such as bears, have a broader diet. Members of this order are commonly called carnivores, although this term is also sometimes used to describe meat-eaters from other orders.

Red fox

European badger

Otter

▲ 3. FAMILY

Related genera are grouped together into families. Mustela is one of 24 genera, including otters and badgers, in the mustelid family (Mustelidae). All are active foragers that seek out prey, with some venturing into water or up trees in search of food.

▲ 2. GENUS

A genus (plural genera) is a group of species that are closely related but cannot breed together. The genus Mustela contains 16 species, including the least weasel, stoat, polecat, and mink. All are small, fierce predators, and each has its own slightly different lifestyle.

Stoat

1. SPECIES ▶

The least weasel has the scientific name Mustela nivalis, made up of the names of its genus (Mustela) and its species (nivalis). Each species has a two-part name like this that is understood by people worldwide. Members of the same species share similar features and can breed with each other in the wild.

Least weasel

INVERTEBRATES

Around 97 percent of animal species are invertebrates. Unlike vertebrates, they lack a backbone. The groups of invertebrate animals are diverse and have little in common. However, all share similar needs. They have to move, take in food and oxygen to supply energy, respond to their surroundings, and reproduce. In this snapshot of selected invertebrates, you can see the body organs and systems that meet these needs in three different types of invertebrate—flatworms, starfish, and lobsters.

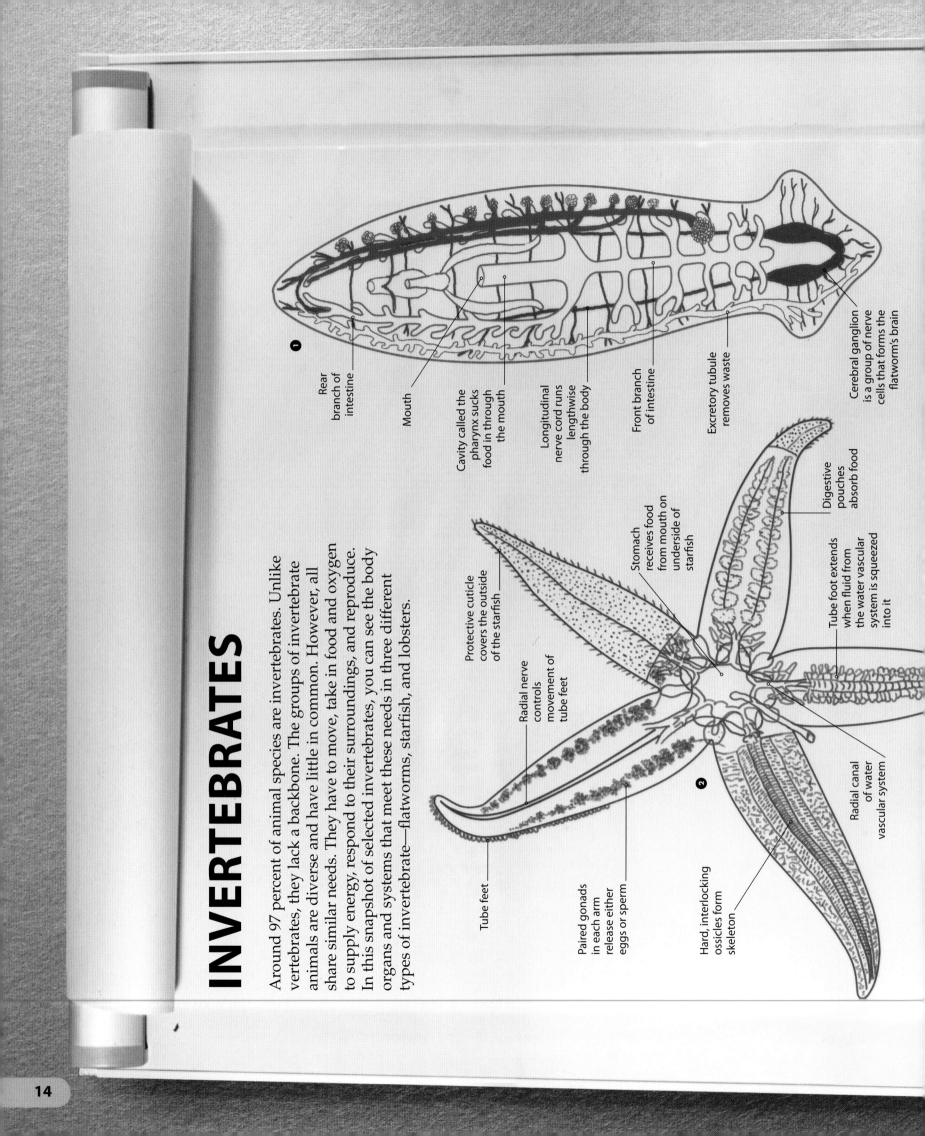

①

Rear branch of intestine

Mouth

Cavity called the pharynx sucks food in through the mouth

Longitudinal nerve cord runs lengthwise through the body

Front branch of intestine

Excretory tubule removes waste

Cerebral ganglion is a group of nerve cells that forms the flatworm's brain

Protective cuticle covers the outside of the starfish

Radial nerve controls movement of tube feet

Stomach receives food from mouth on underside of starfish

Digestive pouches absorb food

Tube foot extends when fluid from the water vascular system is squeezed into it

Tube feet

Paired gonads in each arm release either eggs or sperm

Hard, interlocking ossicles form skeleton

Radial canal of water vascular system

②

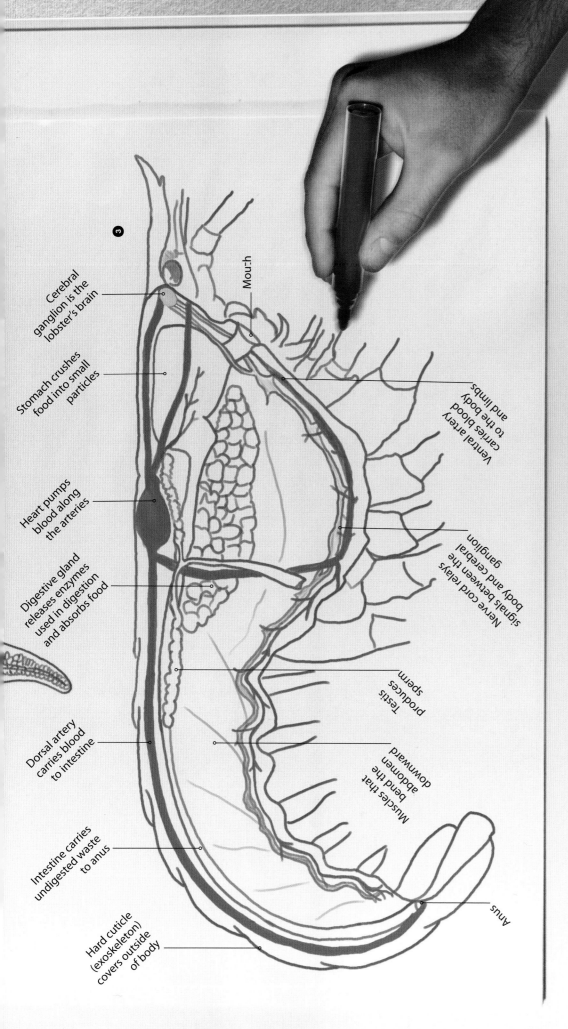

Cerebral ganglion is the lobster's brain

Stomach crushes food into small particles

Heart pumps blood along the arteries

Digestive gland releases enzymes used in digestion and absorbs food

Dorsal artery carries blood to intestine

Intestine carries undigested waste to anus

Hard cuticle (exoskeleton) covers outside of body

Mouth

Ventral artery carries blood to the body and limbs

Nerve cord relays signals between the body and cerebral ganglion

Testis produces sperm

Muscles that bend the abdomen downward

Anus

❶ FLATWORM

These simple invertebrates have neither respiratory (breathing) nor circulatory (blood) systems. Instead, oxygen is taken in directly through the flatworm's surface. Food enters—and undigested food exits—through the mouth, and is distributed to all body parts by the digestive system's many branches. A simple brain controls movement through nerve cords and picks up signals from the simple eyes.

❷ STARFISH

Each arm on this cutaway diagram of a starfish (a type of echinoderm) shows a different layer of the creature's insides. A skeleton of hard ossicles (small bones) lies just under skin. The digestive system consists of a mouth, stomach, and five sets of digestive pouches, one for each arm. Also projecting into each arm is a branch of the water vascular system, which pumps fluid into tiny tube feet, enabling the starfish to move.

❸ LOBSTER

A lobster is an arthropod, with a hard, jointed body, and limbs that are moved by muscles. These are controlled by the brain, which sends signals along a nerve cord. The brain also allows the lobster to see and feel. Food is digested by the digestive system—a tube with openings at each end (the mouth and anus). Blood pumped by the heart through blood vessels and body spaces distributes food and oxygen.

VERTEBRATES

Fish, amphibians, reptiles, birds, and mammals are called vertebrates because they have a vertebral column, or backbone. This is the part of an internal skeleton that supports the skull and to which the limbs are attached. Aside from the skeleton, several other body systems interact to produce a working vertebrate. Most are described here, using the rabbit as an example.

Inside view of a female rabbit with the digestive system unraveled

Neck muscles move and support the head

Outer ear flap channels sounds into inner part of ear

Eye detects light and sends signals to the brain

Nerve carries signals to and from face

① SKIN, HAIR, AND CLAWS

All vertebrates have an outer skin. In fish and reptiles the skin is covered by scales, in birds it is covered by feathers, and in mammals, such as the rabbit, by hair or fur. Hair grows from the skin and helps insulate the animal so it can keep its internal temperature constant. Claws, and related structures such as hooves, are made from the same substance as hair, and help mammals grip the ground as they move.

④ RESPIRATION

During respiration, air is drawn into the lungs. Here, oxygen from the air passes into the bloodstream and is carried to the animal's cells, where it is used to release energy from food. Waste carbon dioxide is carried back to the lungs and breathed out.

⑤ NERVOUS SYSTEM

The nervous system controls the rabbit's movements and enables it to sense its surroundings. Located inside the skull, the brain is the control center of the nervous system, aided by the long spinal cord that connects to its base. Cablelike nerves attached to the brain and spinal cord relay signals to and from all parts of the body.

② SKELETON

The bones of the skeleton form a flexible framework that supports the rabbit, protects its internal organs, and enables it to move. Where two or more bones meet they form a joint, and most of the skeleton's joints are freely movable.

③ CIRCULATION

Blood carries oxygen, food, and other essentials to all parts of the body, and removes waste for disposal. The heart pumps oxygen-rich blood to the body along tubes called arteries. Oxygen-poor blood returns to the heart through veins.

⑥ DIGESTIVE SYSTEM

Food is essential for life since it supplies both energy and building materials. The digestive system consists of a long tube—including the mouth, stomach, and intestines—that digests (breaks down) food into simple, useful nutrients, absorbs those nutrients into the bloodstream, and then gets rid of undigested waste.

Small intestine digests food and absorbs the end products

Appendix is a store of food-digesting bacteria

①

⑦ URINARY SYSTEM

Two kidneys, the bladder, and the tubes that connect them make up the urinary system. The kidneys filter blood to remove wastes and excess water. These form urine that is stored in the baglike bladder before being released from the body.

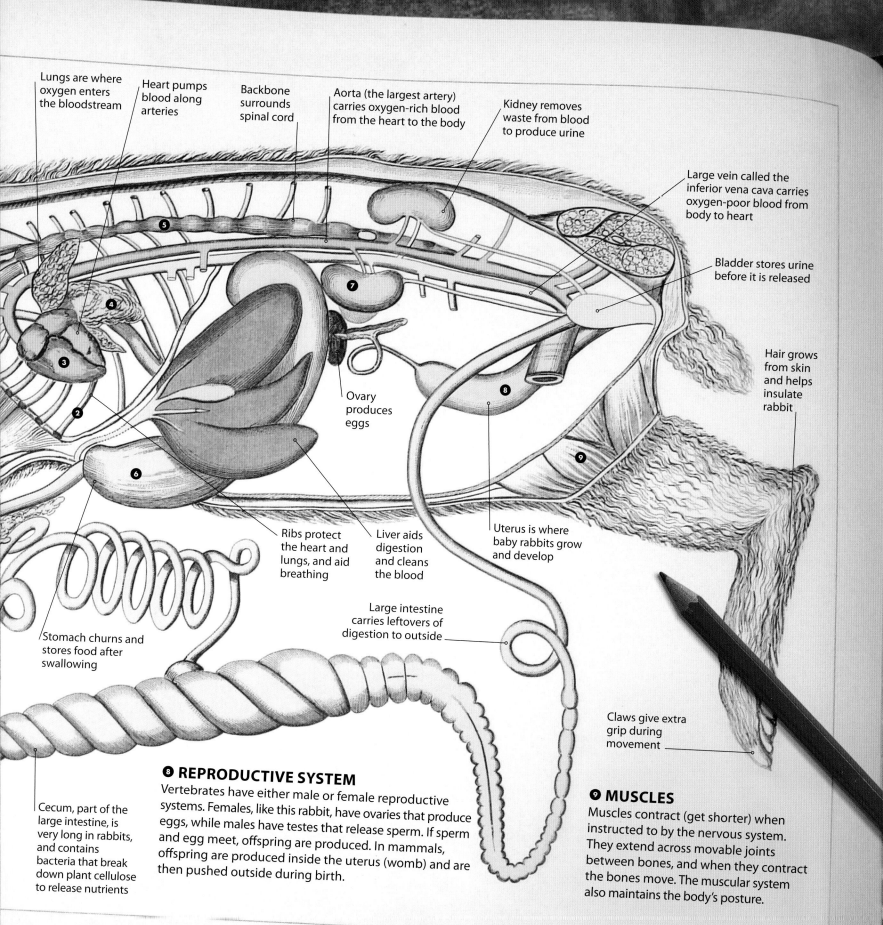

Lungs are where oxygen enters the bloodstream

Heart pumps blood along arteries

Backbone surrounds spinal cord

Aorta (the largest artery) carries oxygen-rich blood from the heart to the body

Kidney removes waste from blood to produce urine

Large vein called the inferior vena cava carries oxygen-poor blood from body to heart

Bladder stores urine before it is released

Hair grows from skin and helps insulate rabbit

Ovary produces eggs

Ribs protect the heart and lungs, and aid breathing

Liver aids digestion and cleans the blood

Uterus is where baby rabbits grow and develop

Large intestine carries leftovers of digestion to outside

Stomach churns and stores food after swallowing

Claws give extra grip during movement

Cecum, part of the large intestine, is very long in rabbits, and contains bacteria that break down plant cellulose to release nutrients

❽ REPRODUCTIVE SYSTEM

Vertebrates have either male or female reproductive systems. Females, like this rabbit, have ovaries that produce eggs, while males have testes that release sperm. If sperm and egg meet, offspring are produced. In mammals, offspring are produced inside the uterus (womb) and are then pushed outside during birth.

❾ MUSCLES

Muscles contract (get shorter) when instructed to by the nervous system. They extend across movable joints between bones, and when they contract the bones move. The muscular system also maintains the body's posture.

Chiton

Shell made of overlapping plates

Nautilus

Cutaway shell reveals chambers

▲ MOLLUSK SHELLS

Made of calcium carbonate, mollusk shells vary greatly. The chiton's flat, jointed shell protects it when attached to a rock, but also allows it to roll into a ball. The nautilus has a spiral shell with gas-filled chambers that help it float.

FLUID SKELETON ▶

Segmented worms, such as leeches and earthworms, have no hard skeleton. Instead, an internal fluid-filled tube, called a hydrostatic skeleton, provides support.

Leech

Forelimbs modified to form wings

BIRD ▶

A bird's skeleton is adapted for flight, and not just by having wings. Hollow bones reduce the skeleton's weight, an enlarged breastbone, or keel, anchors wing-moving muscles, and strong hind limbs aid takeoff and landing.

Crow

Keel provides an anchor for flight muscles

Turtle

Bony layer of external skeleton

SKELETONS

Most animals have a skeleton—a framework that shapes bodies, protects internal organs, and provides anchorage for muscles. Vertebrates have an internal skeleton that is usually made of bone and consists of a backbone attached to a skull and two pairs of limbs. Insects, crustaceans, and other arthropods have a hard external skeleton or exoskeleton. Worms and some echinoderms have a hydrostatic skeleton, which consists of a fluid-filled cavity controlled by muscles.

Large claws moved by strong muscles

Common lobster

▼ EXOSKELETON

Crustaceans, arachnids, and insects have exoskeletons that encase their body and limbs. Plates of hard, light chitin meet at joints to provide flexibility. The exoskeleton cannot expand, so must be molted (shed) to allow growth.

Crustacean cuticle (outer layer) reinforced with calcium carbonate

Badger

Tarantula

Spiny spider crab

A group of bones called the pelvic girdle attaches hind limbs to backbone

Dragonfly

Lizard

Fins propel, stabilize, and steer the fish

◄ **BONY FISH**
Fish such as salmon and cod have bony skeletons. Like most fish, their skeletons give them a streamlined shape. Muscles attached to the flexible backbone bend the body from side to side to propel the fish through water.

Atlantic cod

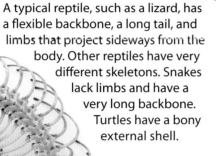

Long, very flexible backbone with many paired ribs

▼ **REPTILE**
A typical reptile, such as a lizard, has a flexible backbone, a long tail, and limbs that project sideways from the body. Other reptiles have very different skeletons. Snakes lack limbs and have a very long backbone. Turtles have a bony external shell.

Tapered skull reduces drag as fish swims through water

Dogfish

Python

Tail fin propels fish forward

CARTILAGINOUS FISH ▶
Sharks (like this dogfish), rays, and skates are called cartilaginous fish because they have an internal skeleton made from cartilage—the same tough, flexible material that supports the human nose and ear.

Fused bones of skull protect brain

Bullfrog

Rhesus monkey

Curved ribs form protective cage around heart and lungs

Long hind limbs and feet for jumping and swimming

Joints between bones give skeleton flexibility

Elongated arm and hand bones support wing

Bat

▲ **MAMMAL**
Most mammals walk on four legs. A strong, curved backbone provides the main axis of the body, and supports the skull. Fore and hind limbs project vertically downward, acting as flexible struts to keep the body off the ground.

SYMMETRY

The bodies of most animals show symmetry (balanced proportions). Some show radial symmetry, meaning they can be divided, like a cake, through a central point into two identical halves. Most animals are bilaterally symmetrical—they can be divided down their midline into two equal halves. Other animals have features that make them look strangely lopsided.

ASYMMETRY ▶

One group of animals, the sponges, lacks any sort of symmetry. These simple animals grow in a random fashion. Their asymmetric structure, cut in any direction, will not produce equal halves.

BILATERAL SYMMETRY ▼

From butterflies to buffalo, most animals show bilateral symmetry. This means that an imaginary line drawn along their length would divide them into identical left and right halves, each with front and back ends. A line anywhere else, however, would not produce equal halves.

Blue morpho butterfly

Head includes eyes, nose, whiskers, and mouth

Weddell seal

Right side of flounder is now its upper surface

▲ HEADS

Animals that are bilaterally symmetrical have a front end called the head. This contains the animal's sense organs, such as the eyes, ears, nose, and whiskers, which meet the environment before the rest of the body. They detect changes, which the brain, also contained in the head, analyzes and responds to.

Left eye has migrated over to the right (upper) side

Agrias claudina butterfly

Body can be divided into two equal halves

Red finger sponge

Giant green anemone

Ring of tentacles around central mouth

Five arms radiate from center

Sponge grows fixed to a reef, rock, or the seabed

RADIAL SYMMETRY ▲
Sea anemones and their relatives show radial symmetry. Their body parts are arranged, like a bicycle wheel, around a central point. Any line drawn through the center divides the animal into two equal halves. Starfish have a special type of radial symmetry, with body parts arranged around the center in five equal sections.

Scarlet starfish

Fiddler crab

Male crab has one claw much larger than the other

LARGE CLAW ▲
Male fiddler crabs look lopsided because one of their claws is much bigger than the other. They raise this claw into the air and wave it around to attract females during courtship. Males also fight claw-to-claw to defend their mudflat burrows against other crabs.

Flounder

SPIRAL SHELL ▶
Most snails are not really symmetrical. They have spiral shells that protects their bodies and internal organs. The shell is a portable retreat into which the snail can withdraw if danger threatens.

Spiral shell encloses twisted body

Snail

◀ CHANGING SIDES
Adult flatfish, such as this flounder, have an unusual symmetry. When it hatches, the flounder is bilaterally symmetrical, but shortly afterward a dramatic change takes place. The eye on the fish's left side migrates to rest next to the right eye. The fish moves to the seabed, where it will now live, and rests on its left side, now its underside.

LIFE SPANS

Usually, the bigger an animal is, the longer its life span. But other factors are also involved. Animals that breed slowly, produce fewer offspring, and show parental care tend to live longer, as do animals with a large brain in relation to their body size, those that consume energy slowly, and those with fewer predators.

❷ **Honeybee workers** are sterile females that fulfill many roles within the bee colony. During their five hectic weeks of life they feed and clean bee larvae and pupae, construct new wax combs for eggs and honey, guard the entrance to the colony, and collect pollen and nectar from flowers.

❶ **Kangaroos** live for 10 years on average. They become mature within two years and are able to breed all year round. Young kangaroos may be preyed on by dingos and birds of prey.

5 WEEKS

10 YEARS

30 YEARS

120 YEARS

400 YEARS

15 YEARS

15 YEARS

12 YEARS

❸ **Giant salamanders** have fairly long lives; they are big amphibians with low energy consumption.

❹ **Sea lions**, preyed upon by large sharks and killer whales, live for 15 years, on average.

❺ **Giant tortoises** live for a lengthy 120 years. Many factors contribute to their staying power: they are big creatures, they live on islands where there are few natural predators, and they are slow-moving, low energy consumers.

❻ **Lobsters** are among the largest crustaceans, protected from predators by their large claws and hard shell. Most live for around 15 years, but exceptional specimens can reach more than 100 years old.

❼ **Domestic cats** live long lives, with shelter, regular feeding, and protection against infection. Animals kept as pets generally live longer than those in the wild because they are fed and protected from predators.

8 Crocodiles are large, ectothermic (cold-blooded) creatures that feed occasionally during brief periods of intense activity but otherwise spend much time immobile—an ideal strategy for a long life.

75 YEARS

9 Bottlenose dolphins are intelligent creatures that, in exceptional cases, can live to 40 or 50 years.

20 YEARS

10 Albatrosses are large ocean birds that take years to become mature. They mate for life and produce just one egg during each breeding season.

50 YEARS

11 Lake sturgeon females take more than 20 years to reach maturity, and only breed every five years.

80 YEARS

12 Polar bears live for an average of 25 years in their harsh Arctic habitat.

25 YEARS

13 Mice are small endothermic (warm-blooded) mammals with a high metabolic rate—a rapid energy consumption for their size. Animals like this tend to "burn out" faster and have shorter life spans.

2 YEARS

6 HOURS

4 WEEKS

40 YEARS

14 Elephants are large, intelligent, social animals that look after their young. They live for around 40 years.

15 House flies have short lives, during which they feed and breed to produce another fly generation.

16 Ocean quahogs are bivalve mollusks (mollusks with two shells). Specimens collected off Iceland in 2007 were found to be more than 400 years old, making them the longest lived animals ever recorded.

17 Mayflies spend two to three years as nymphs feeding in streams and rivers. In summer they emerge as winged adults. They mate but do not feed, and die after just a few hours.

MAMMALS

They may appear very different, but all the animals shown here are mammals, a group that also includes humans. Mammals are endothermic (warm-blooded) vertebrates, and most are covered with insulating fur. Female mammals produce milk to feed their young. Mammals are found almost everywhere on Earth—from the poles to the equator—living on land, in water, and in the air. Most give birth to well-developed young.

Bottlenose dolphin

❶ Streamlined body adapted for life in the water

❶ CETACEANS
Whales, porpoises, and dolphins are cetaceans—mammals that spend their entire lives in water. They have a hairless body propelled by a powerful tail fin and steered by front flippers. Cetaceans include the blue whale, the largest animal that has ever lived.

❷ CARNIVORES
These mammals are hunters and scavengers that feed largely on meat. Carnivores include tigers and other members of the cat family, along with wolves, foxes, otters, and bears. Most are fast-moving, locate prey using their good senses of sight, smell, and hearing, and have sharp teeth to grip and cut flesh.

Tiger

❷

❸ MARSUPIALS
These pouched mammals are found in Australasia and the Americas, and include kangaroos, koalas, and opossums. Female marsupials give birth to tiny, immature young that complete their development inside their mother's pouch.

❸

Kangaroo

❹

❹ ODD-TOED UNGULATES
Ungulates walk on the tips of their toes, each of which is capped with a hard hoof. Odd-toed ungulates have either one or three working toes, and include rhinos, horses, zebras, and tapirs. All are herbivores and many species are fast movers that live on open plains.

❺ LAGOMORPHS
Rabbits and hares are lagomorphs—fast-moving ground-dwellers that eat grasses, soft shoots, and tree bark. Their large ears are highly sensitive, and their bulging eyes provide all-around vision. At the first sound or sight of danger, they use their long hind legs to escape predators.

❺

Long hind legs and feet used like springs to hop at high speeds over long distances

Baby rhinoceros

Hooves are made of keratin, the same material found in human hair and nails

Rat

⑫

Rabbit

African elephant

6 BATS

The only flying mammals, bats are generally nocturnal. The majority are small insect-eaters like the bumblebee-sized Kitti's hog-nosed bat—the world's smallest mammal. Bigger fruit bats eat fruit and nectar, and find food using their large eyes.

Fruit bat

Wing membrane stretches across long finger bones

7 ELEPHANTS

The three species of elephant—two in Africa, one in Asia—are the largest land animals. Elephants are sociable animals that live in family groups and use their trunks to communicate through smell and touch.

Trunk is an extension of the nose that grasps vegetation and transfers it to the mouth

Deer

8 EVEN-TOED UNGULATES

This group of hoofed mammals, including deer, cattle, camels, hippos, and pigs, usually have two hoof-tipped toes. These herbivores have large cheek teeth to grind tough vegetation and may also have large, four-chambered stomachs inside which bacteria aid the digestion of tough plants.

9 PRIMATES

This group includes apes, monkeys, lemurs, bush babies—and humans. Most primates live in social groups in tropical and subtropical forests. The majority are agile climbers with long limbs and flexible, grasping fingers and toes. Primates also have forward-facing eyes and large brains compared to their body size.

10 MONOTREMES

Found in Australasia, echidnas and the duck-billed platypus are monotremes—the only mammals to lay eggs. After hatching, their young feed on milk. The platypus is a good swimmer and probes for prey in the beds of streams and lakes. Spiky echidnas mostly feed on ants and termites.

11 INSECTIVORES

Insects and other small animals are the preferred prey of these mammals. Insectivores are typically small, solitary, nocturnal animals that have sharp teeth and depend on their senses of smell and touch to find food. They include shrews and hedgehogs. Moles are insectivores adapted for life underground.

12 RODENTS

With more than 2,000 species, rodents form the largest mammal group and are found everywhere except Antarctica. Rodents include mice, rats, squirrels, beavers, and porcupines. To gnaw tough foods they have two pairs of sharp incisor (front) teeth, which do not wear down because they never stop growing.

Baboon

Mole

Echidna

BIRDS

The ability to fly means that birds have been able to occupy an incredible range of habitats, including cliff faces, rain-forest canopies, and mountainsides. Birds have streamlined, lightweight bodies with wings that are covered and insulated by feathers. Their toothless beaks vary in shape and size according to their diet and feeding method. The near 10,000 species of birds are divided into 29 orders, most of which are represented here.

▲ **WOODPECKERS**
Tree-dwelling woodpeckers use their strong beaks as chisels to carve out tree holes and to probe for food. Their order includes toucans.

▲ **TROGONS**
Found in tropical forests worldwide, trogons have brilliantly colored feathers and feed mainly on insects.

▲ **PENGUINS**
These flightless seabirds use their wings as flippers to propel their streamlined bodies through the water in pursuit of fish and squid.

▲ **KIWIS**
Ostriches (the world's biggest birds), emus, and kiwis are flightless birds. Over time they have lost the ability to fly, so they run to escape predators.

▲ **TINAMOUS**
These ground-dwelling birds, found in the grasslands of South America, are well camouflaged, have small wings, and are fast fliers and runners.

▲ **HUMMINGBIRDS**
Long-beaked, multicolored hummingbirds hover in front of flowers to feed on nectar. Their close relatives, swifts, spend their lives in the air feeding on insects.

▲ **TURKEYS**
Living on the ground and rarely flying, turkeys belong to the game birds, an order that also includes pheasants and peacocks.

▲ **GREBES**
With a small head and thin neck to make diving easy, grebes are strong swimmers and live on sheltered lakes.

▲ **SWANS**
Together with ducks and geese, swans are waterfowl—excellent swimmers with large, webbed feet.

▲ **KINGFISHERS**
With a daggerlike beak, a kingfisher sits waiting on its riverside perch then dives into the water and grabs a fish.

▲ **DOVES**
Pigeons and doves are plump, strong fliers, with heads that bob up and down when they walk.

▶ **PELICANS**
These birds, from the same order as gannets and tropic birds, scoop up fish in their pouched beaks.

▶ **THRUSHES**
Thrushes belong to the vast order of perching songbirds that contains more than half of all bird species.

▶ **HERONS**
With long legs adapted to wading in shallow water, herons use their long beaks to capture fish and frogs.

▶ **CRANES**
The tallest flying birds in the world, long-legged cranes belong to an order that also includes coots and moorhens.

▶ **GULLS**
Gulls and terns are seabirds, but other members of their order feed by the water's edge.

▶ **ROADRUNNERS**
Members of the cuckoo family, roadrunners live mainly on the ground, running fast to flush out prey and avoid predators.

▶ **ALBATROSSES**
Albatrosses migrate vast distances over the oceans, returning each year to the same breeding sites on land.

▶ **OWLS**
Nighttime hunters, owls have excellent hearing and vision to detect and swoop on prey.

▶ **BIRDS OF PREY**
Eagles and other birds of prey are formidable hunters with excellent eyesight, sharp talons to grab prey, and hooked, tearing beaks.

▶ **NIGHTJARS**
These long-winged birds and their relatives roost in trees or on the ground during the day, then hunt for insects between dusk and dawn.

▶ **FLAMINGOS**
Tall waders with long legs and necks, most flamingos live in flocks in tropical lakes, where they bend their necks to filter animals and plants from the water with their upturned beaks.

▶ **PARROTS**
These forest birds are strong climbers and fliers that feed on fruit and nuts.

DIVERS ▶
Also called loons, streamlined divers make excellent underwater swimmers but find it difficult to walk on land.

27

REPTILES

Alligators, cobras, tortoises, and geckos are just some of the animals found in this diverse group of vertebrates. Most reptiles live on land, and all have tough, scaly skin that stops them from drying out, even in hostile desert habitats. Many lay eggs with leathery shells, although some produce live young. Reptiles are ectothermic (cold-blooded). They bask in the Sun's heat to warm up and seek shade to cool down.

Jackson's chameleon

Male uses horns to fight other males over territory

American alligator

Adhesive foot pads enable gecko to cling to any surface

Tokay gecko

Mangrove snake

Strong jaws snap shut and teeth grip prey

Nile crocodile

Komodo dragon

Powerful, flat-sided tail lashes from side to side to propel crocodile through water

Green anolis

Corn snake

Powerful limbs ending in sharp claws

Pit organs detect heat given off by prey at night to create a "heat picture"

Toxic bacteria in saliva cause blood poisoning in prey

Royal python

Snake-necked turtle

Desert tortoise

Flying gecko

❶ CROCODILIANS

These large, ferocious predators include crocodiles and alligators. They wait in rivers and lakes, then use their powerful jaws and sharp teeth to grab and drown unwary animals. Their eyes and nostrils are set on top of the head so they can see and breathe while in the water.

❷ LIZARDS

More than half of the 8,000 reptile species are lizards. Most are agile, fast-moving hunters. They include geckos, skinks, chameleons, slow worms, the Komodo dragon, and the venomous Gila monster.

❸ VENOMOUS SNAKES

All snakes are carnivorous, and around one-tenth, including adders, cobras, and rattlesnakes, immobilize prey by injecting venom, or poison, through special teeth called fangs.

❹ NONVENOMOUS SNAKES

Many snakes do not use venom. Constrictors, such as corn snakes and pythons, grab their quarry using sharp teeth, then wrap themselves around it and squeeze ever tighter until the animal suffocates. Then, like all snakes, they swallow their victim whole.

❺ TURTLES AND TORTOISES

The bodies of these reptiles are protected by a hard shell. Turtles live in the sea and fresh water, while tortoises live on land. All lay their eggs on land, with marine species migrating across oceans to do so. They lack teeth but their jaws have sharp edges to cut food.

❻ TUATARAS

These burrowing reptiles are found on islands off New Zealand, the sole survivors of an ancient group related to snakes and lizards. They are nocturnal and can live for more than 100 years.

❼ WORM LIZARDS

These wormlike reptiles live in hotter parts of the world. Most have no limbs, and all burrow underground, pushing through soil or sand using their blunt-shaped heads. Worm lizards have fairly simple eyes and feed on insects and worms that they find by touch.

Skin along the sides of the body spreads out to allow lizard to glide

Brown and yellow markings camouflage the puff adder in its grassland habitat

Puff adder

Common iguana

Plumed basilisk lizard

Forked tongue "tastes" chemical particles in the air

Skink

Thorny devil

Sharp, protective spines collect water at night

Gila monster

Slowworm

As the snake strikes, hollow fangs swing forward to inject venom

Green tree python

Rattlesnake

Venom ejected from cobra's mouth can blind an attacker

Red spitting cobra

Tuatara

Worm lizard

Madagascar day gecko

Long tongue used to lick lidless eye clean

❻

❼

29

AMPHIBIANS

Most amphibians spend part of their lives on land and part in water, where they mate and breed. Females lay shell-less eggs, which hatch into swimming larvae called tadpoles that breathe using gills. As they grow into adults, amphibians develop lungs and they can also breathe through their skin. There are three groups of amphibians—the frogs and toads, the salamanders and newts, and the less familiar caecilians.

Webbing between outstretched toes allows frog to glide between trees

Flying frog

Goliath bullfrog

❸

Brazilian gold frog

Smooth skin is moist and lacks scales

Asian horned toad

Poison dart frog

Leopard frog

Male carries string of eggs wrapped around its hind legs

Midwife toad

European common frog

Leopard frog

Frog tadpoles

❷ NEWTS

Newts have long slender bodies and their tails are often flattened to assist movement in water, where many adult newts spend much of their lives. Some newts carry out courtship displays, such as tail swishing, to attract a mate during the breeding season.

❶ MUDPUPPIES

These North American salamanders spend their entire lives underwater. Unlike most other salamanders, mudpuppies retain their bright red external gills into adulthood. They live in streams and rivers, where they feed on fish, crayfish, and mollusks.

Tail moves from side to side to propel newt forward

Great-crested newt

❷

❶

Mudpuppy

External gills

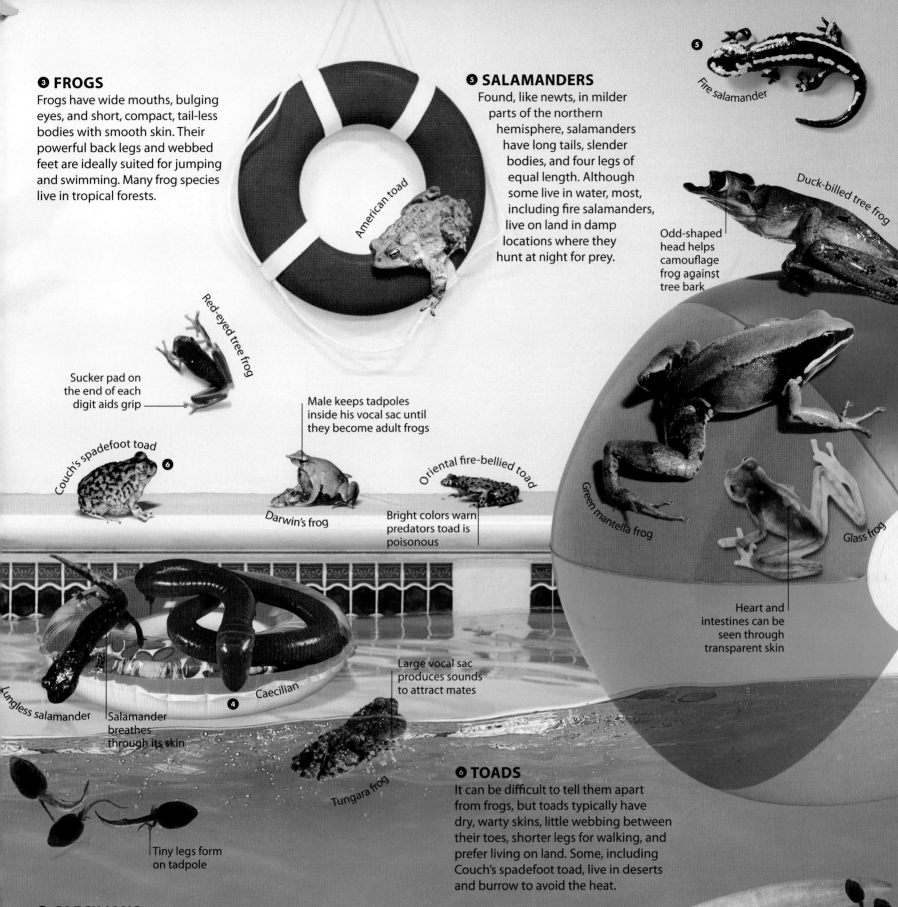

❸ FROGS

Frogs have wide mouths, bulging eyes, and short, compact, tail-less bodies with smooth skin. Their powerful back legs and webbed feet are ideally suited for jumping and swimming. Many frog species live in tropical forests.

American toad

❺ SALAMANDERS

Found, like newts, in milder parts of the northern hemisphere, salamanders have long tails, slender bodies, and four legs of equal length. Although some live in water, most, including fire salamanders, live on land in damp locations where they hunt at night for prey.

❺ Fire salamander

Duck-billed tree frog

Odd-shaped head helps camouflage frog against tree bark

Red-eyed tree frog

Sucker pad on the end of each digit aids grip

Male keeps tadpoles inside his vocal sac until they become adult frogs

Couch's spadefoot toad ❻

Darwin's frog

Oriental fire-bellied toad

Bright colors warn predators toad is poisonous

Green mantella frog

Glass frog

Heart and intestines can be seen through transparent skin

Lungless salamander

Salamander breathes through its skin

Caecilian ❹

Large vocal sac produces sounds to attract mates

Tungara frog

❻ TOADS

It can be difficult to tell them apart from frogs, but toads typically have dry, warty skins, little webbing between their toes, shorter legs for walking, and prefer living on land. Some, including Couch's spadefoot toad, live in deserts and burrow to avoid the heat.

Tiny legs form on tadpole

❹ CAECILIANS

These legless, wormlike amphibians are found in hot, humid places. Some live underwater. Others use their pointed heads to burrow into mud, where their keen sense of smell helps them detect earthworms and other prey, which they grab using their sharp teeth.

External gills

Blind olm lives in dark, watery depths of underground caves

Olm salamander

Hammerhead shark

Bright markings break up fish's outline and confuse predators

Emperor angelfish

FISH

Found in oceans, lakes, and rivers, fish are vertebrates that are adapted for life in water. They have streamlined bodies covered with protective scales, and fins that propel and steer. The three types of fish are jawless fish, such as lampreys; cartilaginous fish, such as sharks and rays; and bony fish, the biggest and most diverse group, which includes most of those swimming here.

Seahorse

Body covered with bony plates

Barracuda

Thick, heavy scales cover the coelacanth's body

5 Coelacanth

2 Anglerfish

Lamprey

3

Lionfish

4

1 SHARK
Found in oceans worldwide, these formidable predators have keen senses, powerful bodies covered with denticles (small toothlike skin growths), rigid fins, and rows of sharp teeth.

2 ANGLERFISH
A growth projecting from the anglerfish's head lures curious prey close to the fish's mouth, which opens wide to consume the visitor whole.

3 LAMPREY
This blood-sucking fish is one of the few survivors of the most ancient group of fish, the jawless fish. It has smooth, scaleless skin and a suckerlike mouth lined with rows of teeth, which it uses to clamp onto the side of a living fish.

4 LIONFISH
This bony fish is one of the most poisonous in the sea. Its long, venomous spines disable predators. Brightly colored stripes warn of the danger.

5 COELACANTH
The coelacanth's fleshy fins are pulled by muscles so it can swim or "walk" over the seabed. Thought to have died out 65 million years ago, it was rediscovered in 1938.

6 RAY
With a mouth on their underside, flat rays feed off creatures on the seabed. They flap their winglike fins to move through the water.

Touch-sensitive barbels used to locate food

7 Sturgeon

9 Anchovies

8 Hatchetfish

Large, upward-pointing eyes detect prey moving overhead

Eyes are located on top of the ray's head

6 Spotted ray

10 Coho salmon

Moray eel **11**

Grouper

7 STURGEON
A long fish with scutes (bony plates) rather than scales, the sturgeon belongs to an ancient group with part-bony and part-cartilage skeletons.

8 HATCHETFISH
This ax-shaped fish lives in the dark ocean midwaters. Light organs on the fish's underside confuse predators by disguising its outline.

9 ANCHOVY
Silvery anchovies feed in shoals on tiny organisms filtered from the water. The dense shoals contain thousands of individuals and attract many predators.

10 SALMON
Like more than 90 percent of the 25,000 species of fish, salmon have bony skeletons and flexible fins. Salmon and their relatives, including trout, are fast-moving carnivores with sharp teeth that ambush prey or attack over a short distance.

11 MORAY EEL
The moray eel lives in tropical waters and has a long, snakelike body that can reach up to 10 ft (3 m) in length. Moray eels ambush their prey. They hide in crevices in rocks and reefs, then launch a surprise attack, grabbing passing prey with their sharp teeth.

ECHINODERMS

These distinctive animals are found only in the sea. Echinoderms, including starfish, sea urchins, and their relatives, have no distinct heads. Instead, the body is divided into five equal parts arranged around a central disk, with the mouth usually on its underside. The body is supported by an internal skeleton made of chalky plates covered by spiny, thin, skin. An internal hydraulic system pumps water into and out of sausagelike tube feet, each tipped with a sucker, that project from the body and are used for movement.

❶ SEA DAISY

These small echinoderms are flattened and disk-shaped, with no arms but a ring of spines around their margin. Their structure is similar to other echinoderms, with a body arranged in five parts. They probably feed on bacteria and microscopic mollusks.

❷ FEATHER STAR

Like their close relatives the sea lilies, plantlike feather stars are usually attached to the sea bottom by a stalk. Some, however, are free-swimming as adults. Feather stars feed by using their arms to transfer food particles from the surrounding water into their central, upward-facing mouth.

❸ STARFISH

Familiar and star-shaped, starfish have five or more arms attached to a central disk. They are scavengers or predators that crawl over the sea bottom using their suckerlike tube feet. They feed by pushing their stomachs out through their mouths to surround food, digest it, and suck up the juices.

❹ BRITTLESTAR

With long, thin arms attached to a small, central disk, brittlestars move by wiggling their arms in a snakelike fashion. To evade predators, the arms can break off and be regrown. Brittlestars feed by scavenging, catching small animals, or filtering particles from the water.

❺ SEA CUCUMBER

Sea cucumbers have more flexible bodies than other echinoderms. They also have a front end, with a mouth, and a back end, with an anus. The mouth is surrounded by tentacles that filter small particles of food from the water. Some species shoot sticky threads out of the anus to deter predators.

❻ SEA URCHIN

A sea urchin's globe-shaped body lacks arms but has a hard outer test or shell. Tube feet project through the test, which is armed with movable spines to deter enemies and aid movement. Sea urchins move slowly over rocks, grazing on algae or eating small animals.

❼ SAND DOLLAR

Close relatives of the sea urchins, sand dollars have irregular, flattened, and inflexible bodies covered by many small spines. Their body shape helps them to burrow easily into soft sand.

CRUSTACEANS

From tiny brine shrimps to large spider crabs, the 50,000 species of crustacean are very diverse and live mainly in the sea and fresh water. Crustaceans have a hard external skeleton, known as the exoskeleton or cuticle, jointed limbs, two pairs of sensory antennae, and compound eyes on stalks. Their heads and thoraxes are often covered by a shield or carapace.

BRANCHIOPODS ▼

These small crustaceans use leaflike limbs for movement, respiration, and to gather food particles. Branchiopods are found mostly in fresh water, although brine shrimps are a species of branchiopod that live in salty lakes and pools. Brine shrimps have a short life cycle and lay eggs that can remain dormant for years.

COPEPODS ▶

Superabundant in the plankton found near the ocean's surface, these tiny crustaceans are also found in fresh water. Copepods have a teardrop-shaped, transparent body, with a single compound eye, and large antennae that, along with the swimming legs, play a part in movement.

Peacock mantis shrimp

Freshwater copepod

Brine shrimp

Pill woodlouse rolling up

WOODLICE ▶

Among the few crustaceans that live on land, woodlice thrive in dark, damp places, such as rotting wood, where they feed on dead plant matter. Their upper surface is protected by tough, curved plates, and females carry their eggs in a special pouch on their undersides.

Woodlice

◀ MANTIS SHRIMP

This ferocious predator is neither a shrimp nor a praying mantis (a type of insect). Its second pair of legs—normally folded away, like those of a praying mantis—are adapted for either spearing or smashing prey. When the mantis shrimp ambushes prey, it shoots out these legs at high speed to kill or dismember its victim.

Crayfish

LOBSTER AND CRAYFISH ▶

Big crustaceans with a hard carapace and long abdomen, lobsters emerge from hiding at night and use their massive claws to crush and cut prey. Lobsters walk over the seabed, but can flip their tails to swim backward. Crayfish resemble small lobsters. They live in freshwater streams and rivers, where they make burrows in silt and mud.

CRABS ▶

Easily identified by their short, broad bodies protected by a hard carapace, most crabs live in the sea, although some prefer fresh water and even land. The first of their five pairs of legs have powerful pincers used to grasp and crush food, for defense, and even for signaling to other crabs. The remaining eight legs enable them to scuttle sideways quickly.

Shore crab

Common lobster

Spider crab

▼ KRILL

Tiny shrimplike krill are found in vast swarms in oceans worldwide. They are an important source of food for many larger marine animals.

Krill

Crayfish

Common shrimp

SHRIMPS ▶

These small bottom-dwellers have a near-transparent, highly flexible exoskeleton. Shrimps use their legs to swim or walk along the seabed. If threatened, they flick their tail downward to dart backward out of harm's way. Most shrimps eat almost anything, including pieces of dead animals plucked using their tiny pincers.

Goose barnacles

BARNACLES ▼

In early life, barnacles swim freely but they soon settle, forming large encrustations on rocks, ships, piers, whales, and even other crustaceans. The body of an adult barnacle is encased by chalky plates and either fixed directly onto a surface or, as in the case of these goose barnacles, attached by a stalk. Barnacles feed by opening the plates and extending feathery legs that filter tiny creatures from the water.

ARACHNIDS

Spiders, scorpions, and other arachnids are mainly land-dwelling predators. Most use venom to disable their prey, then douse it with digestive enzymes and suck up the resulting liquid. The arachnid body has two parts—a cephalothorax at the front and an abdomen at the rear. Attached to the cephalothorax are a pair of fanglike mouthparts called chelicerae, two appendages called pedipalps that are either leglike or clawlike, and four pairs of walking legs. In spiders, the abdomen contains silk-producing glands.

❶ HARVESTMEN

Commonly mistaken for spiders, harvestmen have an oval body with no "waist" between front and rear parts. Harvestmen use their second and longest pair of legs as feelers to find their way and detect prey. They feed on small insects, plants, dead animals, and dung. Some, if threatened, can detach their legs, which continue moving to confuse predators.

Mexican red-rumped tarantula

❶
Harvestman

Huntsman
spider

Cephalothorax,
the front part
of the body

Crab spider

Chelicerae used
to inject venom
into prey

❸ SPIDERS

More than half of arachnid species are spiders. All produce silk threads, which some, such as orb web spiders, use to spin insect-trapping webs. Others, including tarantulas and jumping spiders, stalk their prey.

❻ SCORPIONS

Found in hotter regions, scorpions hunt at night, using special vibration sensors to detect prey. They hold prey in their clawlike pedipalps while picking off small morsels of food using their sharp chelicerae.

❼ WHIP SPIDERS

With broad, flat bodies, these tropical arachnids move sideways, feel for insect prey with their long, thin first legs, then grab it with their pincerlike pedipalps. Whip spiders are nocturnal, and spend the day hiding under stones, in leaf litter, or in caves.

Cave spider

❽ MITES AND TICKS

The smallest of the arachnids, some being barely visible, mites and ticks have rounded, one-piece bodies. Mites are found by the millions in soil and water, and also include parasites of both plants and animals. Ticks feed on the blood of mammals and birds. They penetrate the skin with their barbed mouthparts, expand enormously as they suck blood, and then drop off.

❹ PSEUDOSCORPIONS

Resembling smaller versions of scorpions, pseudoscorpions lack both a tail and sting. They have venom glands in their pedipalps, which they use to immobilize insects and other small prey. Pseudoscorpions hunt for prey in soil, leaf litter, and under logs and rocks.

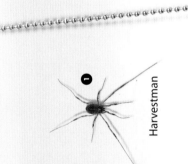

Abdomen,
the rear part
of the body

Funnel web spider

❺ SUN SPIDERS

Also called wind scorpions, these fast-running arachnids are found in deserts. They locate prey with their long, sensitive pedipalps, which they also use to hold prey while they kill and chew it with their pincerlike chelicerae.

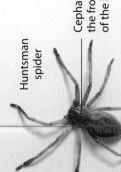
Orb web spider
❸

Spitting
spider

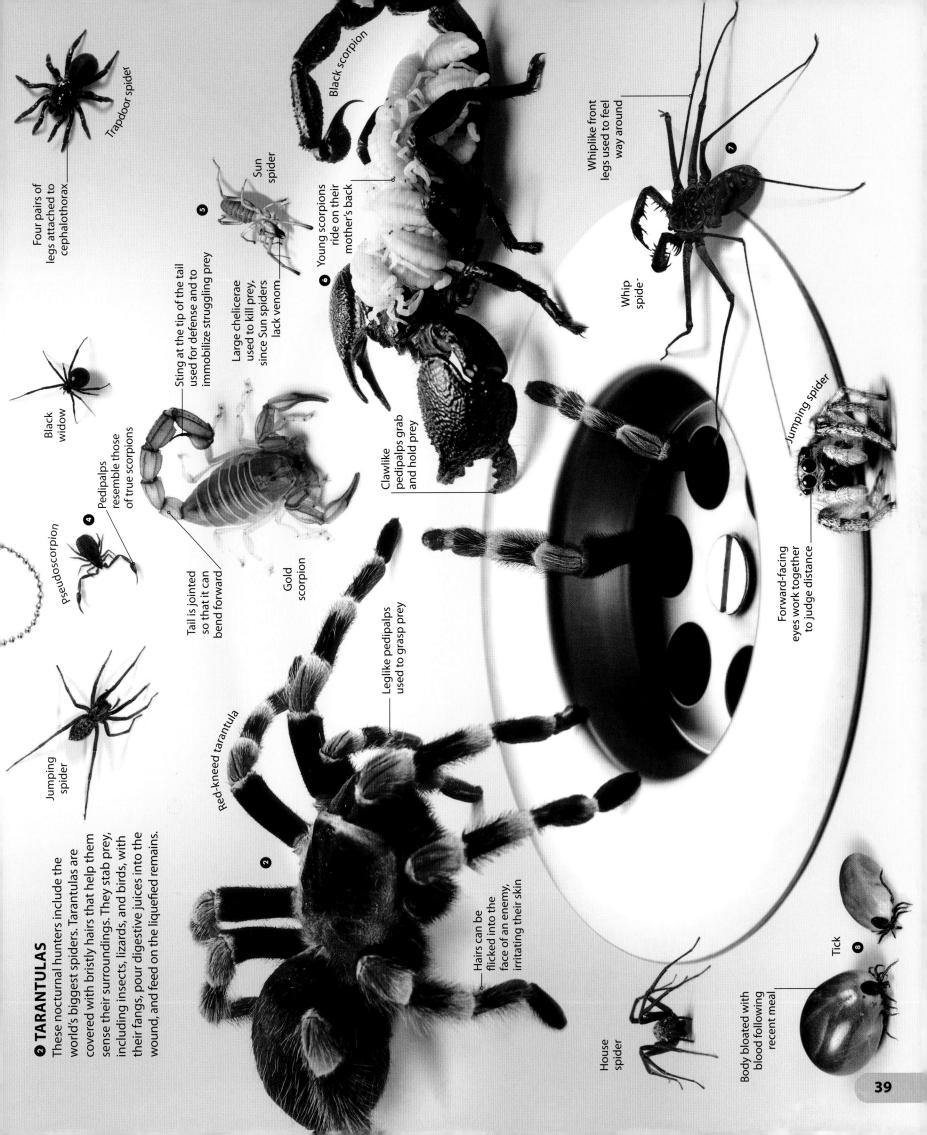

❷ TARANTULAS

These nocturnal hunters include the world's biggest spiders. Tarantulas are covered with bristly hairs that help them sense their surroundings. They stab prey, including insects, lizards, and birds, with their fangs, pour digestive juices into the wound, and feed on the liquefied remains.

Trapdoor spider

Four pairs of legs attached to cephalothorax

Black widow

Jumping spider

❸ Pedipalps resemble those of true scorpions

Pseudoscorpion

Sting at the tip of the tail used for defense and to immobilize struggling prey

Sun spider

❺

Young scorpions ride on their mother's back

❻

Black scorpion

Large chelicerae used to kill prey, since Sun spiders lack venom

Tail is jointed so that it can bend forward

Gold scorpion

Clawlike pedipalps grab and hold prey

Whiplike front legs used to feel way around

❼

Whip spider

Leglike pedipalps used to grasp prey

Red-kneed tarantula

❷

Jumping spider

Forward-facing eyes work together to judge distance

Hairs can be flicked into the face of an enemy, irritating their skin

House spider

Body bloated with blood following recent meal

Tick

❽

39

INSECTS

From bees to butterflies, insects form the most successful animal group on Earth. There are more than one million named insect species, with probably another 10 to 30 million yet to be discovered. An insect body has three parts. The head has two compound eyes and a pair of antennae, the thorax carries three pairs of legs and, usually, two pairs of wings, and the abdomen contains reproductive organs. Insects are found everywhere, except for the oceans.

◀ DRAGONFLIES

These fast-moving predators have alternately beating front and rear wings that allow them to fly through the air with incredible control. Equipped with large eyes, dragonflies use their excellent vision to detect unsuspecting prey, such as flies, then dart in to make the kill.

Southern hawker dragonfly has a slender body and long, thin wings

Southern hawker dragonfly

◀ GRASSHOPPERS AND CRICKETS

Although grasshoppers and crickets have large wings, they usually employ their long hind legs to leap away from danger. All have chewing mouthparts. Grasshoppers and their relatives, such as locusts, are plant-eaters, while crickets are scavengers or omnivores.

Desert locust

Male locusts "sing" to attract females by rubbing hind legs against wings

Flattened body allows cockroach to squeeze into tiny crevices

American cockroach

COCKROACHES ▶

These mainly nocturnal insects are very sensitive to vibrations and scurry for cover if danger threatens. Most common in tropical and subtropical regions, cockroaches are generally scavengers. A few species are pests, infesting homes and feeding on food scraps.

Praying mantis

MANTIDS ▶

Also called praying mantises because of the way they hold their front legs, mantids are solitary predators, with a triangular head and large eyes. Their bodies blend in well with the leaves of forest trees. Mantids stay motionless, waiting for prey to wander within striking distance, then shoot their spiked front legs forward to grab their next meal.

Leaf cutter ants

Two long antennae

Buff-tailed bumblebee

Emerald cockroach wasp

Ichneumon wasp

WASPS, BEES, AND ANTS ▶

These insects have a narrow "waist" between their thorax and abdomen, and, in females, a sting. Many, including wood ants and honeybees, live in large, highly organized colonies, and are important pollinators of flowers.

Cuckoo wasp

Male driver ant

Wings only found on males

▼ BEETLES

With at least 370,000 species, beetles make up the largest group of insects. Their hard front wings form a wing case that folds over and protects the rear wings and abdomen. Beetles are found in fresh water and almost everywhere on land, and they use their biting mouthparts to feed on plants, fungi, other insects, dead animals, or even dung.

Rove beetle

African ground beetle

Golden scarab beetle

Jewel beetle

Leaf weevil

Brightly colored wing case

Darwin's beetle

Male Darwin's beetle has a large set of jaws

Flattened body of violin beetle resembles a violin

▼ BUGS

All bugs have a feeding tube that pierces their food and sucks out the juices. For example, most shield bugs and plant hoppers, such as the well-camouflaged thorn bug, suck sugar-rich sap from plants. Water bugs, such as the backswimmer, are predators of other invertebrates and small fish.

Striped shield bug

Thorn bug

Common backswimmer (water boatman)

Long legs used for swimming

Moth's wings are covered with thousands of tiny scales

African Moon moth

Pericopine moth

▼ FLIES

These agile fliers have just one pair of wings and feed by sucking up liquids. They include nectar-feeders, such as bee flies and crane flies, decomposers that feed on rotting matter, such as houseflies, and predators, such as robber flies, that feed on other insects.

House fly

Crane fly

True flies have just one pair of wings

Robber fly

Bee fly

Asterope sapphira butterfly

BUTTERFLIES AND MOTHS ▶

Butterflies are generally brightly colored and active during the day, while most moths are nocturnal. Both use a long, coiled "tongue" to feed on nectar or other liquids.

Verdant sphinx moth

MOLLUSKS

This amazingly diverse group includes more than 100,000 species, ranging from garden slugs to pearl-bearing oysters and terrifying giant squid. Despite their differences, most mollusks share some common features. They all have a soft body, often protected by a hard, chalky shell, and feed using a roughened strip called a radula. They have a muscular foot for movement and breathe using gills. Most belong to the gastropods—the group that includes snails and slugs.

CEPHALOPODS ▼

Octopuses, squid, nautiluses, cuttlefish, and other cephalopods are intelligent mollusks. They have a large head and a mouth surrounded by arms or tentacles, which are used for movement and catching fish and crabs. The mouth is equipped with a horny beak and a toothed radula for dragging in food. Cephalopods can move very quickly using a form of jet propulsion.

Common squid

Large eyes provide excellent vision

Shell contains chambers that provide buoyancy

Pearly nautilus

Common octopus

Blue giant clam

Suckers used to grip prey

◄ CHITONS

These inhabitants of rocky shores have a flat shell made up of eight overlapping plates. At low tide, chitons cling tightly to rocks and, if pulled off, curl up into a protective ball. At high tide they creep slowly over rocks using their muscular foot and feed on algae and other small organisms by scraping them off the rocky surface with their radula.

Chiton

Troschel's murex

Blue (common) mussels

Valves of shell open to draw in water current

Textile cone shell

Conus pertusus

Cone shell paralyzes prey with its poisonous, harpoonlike radula

BIVALVES ►

Found in both fresh water and the sea, bivalves include clams and mussels. Bivalves have a hinged shell with two pieces or valves. They breathe by drawing a current of water into their shell from which large gills extract oxygen. The gills also trap food particles that are then transferred to the mouth, a process called filter feeding.

Bright colors warn predators that the sea slug is poisonous

Pair of nudibranch sea slugs

TUSK SHELLS ►

With shells that resemble miniature elephant's tusks, these sea-dwelling mollusks are found offshore where they burrow into the seabed. The small eyeless head that emerges from the shell's larger opening is surrounded by small tentacles. These sweep the seabed for tiny particles and draw them into the tusk shell's mouth.

Common limpet

North's long whelk

Hooped whelk

Spiral shell protects soft-bodied whelk

GASTROPODS ►

Most gastropods live in the sea. They have a head with eyes and tentacles, a muscular foot that produces creeping movements and all except the slugs have a large external— and often spiral—shell. Most, including cone shells, whelks, murexes, and sea slugs, are carnivores. Limpets are grazers with a simple cone-shaped shell.

WORMS

The term "worm" is a general one used to describe invertebrates that have long, soft bodies and, usually, no legs. Worms are found in a range of habitats including soil, tropical forests, lakes, rivers, and the sea. Flatworms are the simplest worms and have flattened, ribbonlike bodies. Annelids have bodies divided into segments. Other worm groups include peanut worms and velvet worms.

▼ LEECH

These annelid worms have a flattened body with a sucker at each end. Most live in fresh water, where they swim. Outside of water, they move by attaching their suckers to surfaces and arching their bodies. Some 75 percent of leeches are bloodsuckers. The rest are mostly predators of other invertebrates.

Most segments have tiny bristles called chaetae

▼ PEANUT WORM

Found in burrows in shallow seas, these worms have a slender front end, tipped with a tentacled mouth, and a swollen rear end. If threatened, they can retract their front end into their rear end, making them resemble a peanut shell. Peanut worms feed by filtering particles from sand using their tentacles.

VELVET WORM ▼

Inhabitants of tropical forests, velvet worms have a wormlike body and up to 43 pairs of short, stubby legs with clawed "feet." The head has sensory antennae, jaws, and glands that squirt slime over prey in order to disable it.

Body coated with slippery mucus

▼ LAND PLANARIAN

Flatworms like this one live in habitats with both high temperatures and humidity. They glide over soil or leaves on a thin film of slippery mucus. Land planarians feed on other worms, slugs, and insect larvae that they take in through the mouth in the middle of their underside.

MARINE FLATWORM ▶

Polyclads (marine flatworms) are oval-shaped and often brightly-colored, especially those that live on coral reefs. Bright colors serve as a warning to potential predators that the flatworm tastes bad. Most polyclads are predators that eat smaller invertebrates.

Rippling the edges of the body allows the worm to move

PEACOCK WORM ▶

The peacock worm is a bristleworm—a type of annelid—and lives attached to the sea bottom in a tube it constructs from mucus and sand grains. A feathery "crown" of filaments encircling its mouth traps tiny food particles that drift past. If danger threatens, the worm instantly folds its crown and retreats into its tube.

BEARDED FIREWORM ▼

Like many bristleworms, the bearded fireworm moves using paddlelike lobes, reinforced with bristles, which project from its sides. The bearded fireworm's bristles carry a poison that can cause paralysis if touched. Fireworms live on reefs where they feed on corals, anemones, and small crustaceans.

Each segment carries a pair of lobes with bristles

EARTHWORM ▲

With familiar rounded bodies, earthworms burrow through soil by changing shape. The front part of the body elongates, its tiny bristles gripping the burrow, while the rear part follows. Earthworms are annelids and eat soil, digesting the decaying plant material it contains.

45

Tentacles are colonies of tiny animals

Portuguese man-of-war ❸

Sea nettle

❹

Box jellyfish

Tentacles can inflict lethal stings

Beroid comb jelly

❶

SPONGES, JELLIES, AND CORALS

Some of the simplest members of the animal kingdom belong to three phyla—Porifera, Cnidaria, and Ctenophora. Poriferans are sponges, animals that feed by filtering food from the water. Cnidarians include hydrozoans, jellyfish, corals, and sea anemones. All have stinging tentacles that immobilize and trap prey. Ctenophores, also known as comb jellies, are related to the cnidarians.

❶ COMB JELLIES

Delicate and nearly transparent, comb jellies swim among the ocean plankton. Eight rows of hairlike cilia extend from top to bottom, beating in waves to move the comb jelly around. Most catch prey with two sticky tentacles, but this beroid comb jelly uses its mouth to eat prey whole.

❷ SPONGES

The simplest of all animals, sponges are unlike any other creatures. Most attach themselves to the seabed, where they grow without symmetry, their bodies supported by a "skeleton" made of tiny struts and peppered with pores. Water is drawn into the pores and food particles are filtered out and digested.

❸ HYDROZOANS

This group of cnidarians shows astonishing variety, from animals that resemble tiny sea anemones to the extraordinary Portuguese man-of-war. This jellyfish is not one organism but a colony of cooperating animals. One forms the prominent gas balloon that allows the colony to float and drift. Others make up the tentacles.

❹ JELLYFISH

Scyphozoans or "true" jellyfish have a bell-shaped body, filled with the jellylike substance that gives the animal its name, and prey-catching, stinging tentacles. A jellyfish swims by contracting its body to force out water from its underside and propel it in the opposite direction. Related box jellyfish are notorious for their toxic stings that can kill humans.

❺ SEA ANEMONES

They may look like colorful plants, but sea anemones are predators that eat small animals. On top of the anemone's body is a central mouth surrounded by stinging tentacles. A base fixes the animal to a rock. If threatened, many anemones rapidly expel water from their insides and shrink dramatically.

Yellow tube sponge

Opening through which water current leaves sponge

Sea sponge

❷

Water enters sponge through tiny openings in its surface

❺

Stinging tentacles capture prey, then draw it into central mouth

❻ CORAL

Resembling tiny sea anemones, corals live in vast groups in clear, shallow, tropical waters. They protect themselves by building hard cases of calcium carbonate into which they can withdraw. Over time, the massed cases form huge coral reefs that provide habitats for fish and many other marine animals.

❻

Giant green sea anemone

Carpet anemone

ANCIENT ANIMALS

Around one billion years ago the first animals appeared on Earth. Since that time, a vast array of animal species have evolved, or developed gradually over successive generations. Extinction (when a species dies out) is a natural part of this process, even when whole groups disappear as a result of dramatic changes in their environment. These are just some examples from the history of animal life.

520 MILLION YEARS AGO

Anomalocaris

Opabinia

Opabinia had five eyes.

370 MILLION YEARS AGO

Dunkleosteus

Head of *Dunkleosteus* protected by bony plates

Streamlined body shape allowed *Cladoselache* to move quickly through the water

Cladoselache

265 MILLION YEARS AGO

Dragonfly

▲ 520 MILLION YEARS AGO

Around this time there was a massive explosion in the numbers and types of invertebrates in Earth's warm oceans. *Anomalocaris* was a 2-ft- (60-cm-) long predator that swam using two winglike flaps. *Opabinia* grabbed prey with its long proboscis.

▲ 370 MILLION YEARS AGO

The oceans abounded with many animals, including new types of fish. The placoderms—early fish with jaws—included *Dunkleosteus*, an armored giant that sliced through prey with its razor-sharp toothplates. The earliest sharks included *Cladoselache*, a predator that seized prey and swallowed it whole.

▲ 265 MILLION YEARS AGO

Forests of conifers thrived in warm dry conditions where mammal-like reptiles dominated life on land. One was *Dimetrodon*, a giant predator with a "sail" on its back that helped it to warm up and become active more rapidly. In the air, large dragonflies were the main hunters.

10,000 YEARS AGO

Dimetrodon's sail was used to control body temperature

Woolly mammoth

Giant sloth

▲ 10,000 YEARS AGO
The woolly mammoth and the giant sloth were among the large mammals that lived during the past two million years. All became extinct around 10,000 years ago, because of climate change at the end of the last Ice age and because hunting by people spread across the world.

RECENT HISTORY

Dodo

Thylacine

150 MILLION YEARS AGO

Allosaurus

Pterodactylus

Allosaurus tore its prey apart using its sharp teeth

▲ 150 MILLION YEARS AGO
At this time the climate was warm and dinosaurs dominated life on Earth. They included ferocious, fast-moving carnivores, such as *Allosaurus*, as well as giant, lumbering plant-eaters. Flying reptiles, such as *Pterodactylus*, preyed on smaller animals. By 65 million years ago, both groups were extinct.

RECENT HISTORY ▶
In recent times human activity has accelerated the rate of extinction. The dodo was a flightless bird discovered on Mauritius in 1598. By 1681, introduced cats, rats, and other egg-eaters had made it extinct. The presence of Europeans in Tasmania made the doglike thylacine extinct by the 1930s.

ON THE BRINK

Extinction is a natural part of life on Earth. Over millions of years, some species disappear while new species evolve. Since the 1600s, however, the rate of extinction has risen steadily, with species vanishing as a direct result of human activities. The World Conservation Union lists more than 16,000 animal species on the brink of extinction, including those shown here.

SIBERIAN TIGER ▼

Like other tigers, the Siberian tiger is critically endangered. Tigers are officially protected, but poachers kill them for their skins and for body parts, which are used in traditional Chinese medicine. The tiger's habitat is also shrinking because of intensive logging.

ECHO PARAKEET ▶

In the 1980s, only 10 echo parakeets remained on the Indian Ocean island of Mauritius, due to habitat loss and rats raiding their nests. Since then, however, conservation measures have resulted in a steady rise in the number of parakeets.

▲ PANAMANIAN GOLDEN FROG

Many frog species have gone into decline because of fungal infections. The Panamanian golden frog is no exception. The last specimens in the wild were seen in 2007 and have since been collected for breeding in captivity to save the species.

CALIFORNIA CONDOR ▶

Trapping, shooting, poisoning, and collisions with power lines brought this American vulture near to extinction. In 1987, all 22 surviving birds were taken into captivity, where they were bred successfully. Numbers are now steadily increasing.

AMERICAN BURYING BEETLE ▶

Once widespread across the US, this beetle buries the carcasses of rodents and birds to feed its young. Today, only a few remain, probably because of the use of pesticides (chemicals that kill insect pests) and changes in their habitat.

◀ SAIGA ANTELOPE
Numbers of saiga antelope have decreased by 90 percent since the 1980s. Their horns are used in traditional Chinese medicine. There are now just four isolated populations in the steppes (grasslands) of Russia and central Asia.

OAHU TREE SNAIL ▶
The Hawaiian island of Oahu was once home to 41 species of tree snails. Predation by the rosy wolf snail and loss of their natural habitat made most of them extinct. Today, just two species survive in the wild.

▲ FLOREANA CORAL
This rare species is found around the Galápagos Islands. Since 1982 the extent of the coral has decreased by 80 percent. The causes are believed to be heating of the Pacific Ocean, caused by global warming, and the El Niño effect, a change in ocean currents.

◀ WESTERN LOWLAND GORILLA
One of our closest relatives, this gorilla lives in the tropical forests of western Africa. Numbers have dropped as human populations have increased. Their forest home has been cut down to provide farmland, and people have hunted gorillas for meat. Deadly Ebola fever has killed gorillas and humans alike.

LEATHERBACK TURTLE ▶
The leatherback was once widespread in oceans around the world. Today, it faces a variety of threats. Its eggs, laid in burrows on sandy beaches, are targeted by egg thieves, while adult turtles can be trapped by fishing nets or mistakenly eat discarded plastic bags—which block their digestive system—instead of jellyfish, their natural food.

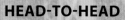

HEAD-TO-HEAD

Two male bison meet head-to-head to establish which is the stronger. Competition is just one of many life skills, such as feeding, communication, and defense, that animals perform daily in order to survive.

Life skills

RESPIRATION

Animals need oxygen to release the energy in their cells that powers all life activities. The energy-liberating process, called cell respiration, also releases waste carbon dioxide. How animals take in oxygen depends on their complexity and habitat. Many animals breathe in oxygen from air or water using structures such as lungs or gills, and have a blood system to carry the oxygen to their cells.

Air sacs connected to lungs

FLATWORM ▶

These simple animals have neither a respiratory system to take in oxygen nor a blood system to carry it to their cells. Instead, a flatworm takes in oxygen and loses carbon dioxide directly through its surface. This is possible because the flatworm, being extremely thin, possesses a very large outer surface through which oxygen can pass.

MOLLUSK ▶

How mollusks take in oxygen depends on their type and habitat. Land snails, slugs, and air-breathing pond snails have a lung. Marine mollusks, including sea slugs and clams, use gills to take in oxygen from the surrounding water, as do octopuses and squid.

AMPHIBIAN LARVA ▶

This newt larva or tadpole—like other young amphibians—depends on feathery external gills to extract oxygen from water. When it becomes an adult newt it will lose its gills and develop lungs.

▼ FISH

Red because of their rich blood supply, a fish's gills are located behind its mouth. The fish draws water into its mouth, across its gills, and back out again. Dissolved oxygen passes into the bloodstream and circulates around the body.

Pond snail

Newt tadpole

Goldfish

Feathery external gills

Flaplike operculum covers gills

▼ BIRD

As active fliers, birds need much more oxygen than mammals, and have a more efficient respiratory system. Nine air sacs work like bellows to maintain a one-way flow of air through the lungs, and to clear any used air quickly.

▼ INSECT

Holes called spiracles in an insect's thorax and abdomen allow air in and out of its body. Spiracles lead to branching tubes called tracheae that carry oxygen-rich air to all parts of the body, and remove carbon dioxide.

Spiracle in the side of a grasshopper's abdomen

MAMMAL ▼

Like other mammals, a hamster has two lungs. The lungs are made up of millions of tiny air sacs, each surrounded by blood capillaries that carry oxygen away. Air is sucked into or squeezed out of the lungs by muscles that make the chest cavity bigger or smaller.

AQUATIC MAMMAL ▲

Whales and other marine mammals have lungs and, unlike fish, cannot extract oxygen from seawater. They must come to the surface to breathe air, although they can wait much longer between breaths than land mammals. A whale has a nostril or nostrils—called a blowhole—on top of its head. When it surfaces, stale air (and any water lodged in the blowhole) is blown out as spray.

AMPHIBIAN ADULT ▶

Once it reaches adulthood, an amphibian, such as this frog, takes in oxygen through its lungs. In order to breathe, the mouth closes and air is drawn through the nostrils and into the lungs. Then the body wall contracts (squeezes) to push air out of the lungs. Frogs also take in oxygen through their moist skin.

FEEDING

Animals eat to survive. They eat a wide range of foods and show many different feeding techniques. Animals are divided into different categories, such as herbivores and carnivores, according to their food preferences. Once an animal has eaten food, it is digested (broken down) to release its essential nutrients. These nutrients supply the energy needed for movement and the raw materials used for growth and repair.

Leopard

❶

❶ CARNIVORES

These animals feed exclusively on meat or fish, food sources rich in nutrients. Carnivores are predators that either hunt or lie in wait for their prey. They include leopards, snakes, bullfrogs, and sea eagles. Many have large teeth and strong jaws, or sharp beaks and talons.

❷ SCAVENGERS

This clean-up squad of flesh-eaters feeds on dead animals. Vultures, for example, are scavenging specialists that use their sharp, hooked beaks to cut through skin and flesh, and their rough tongues to rasp meat from bones.

❸ INSECTIVORES

Animals that feed on insects are called insectivores. The giant anteater, for example, breaks open ant or termite nests using its powerful claws. It flicks its long, sticky tongue in and out of broken nests to scoop up the thousands of insects it needs to eat daily.

American black vulture

❷

Farmyard pig

❺

Vampire bat

❹

Sharp teeth
gnaw nut held
in front paws

Gray squirrel

❸ Giant anteater

Fruit forms the
main part of an
orang-utan's diet

Guinea pig

Narrow snout
housing long
tongue probes
into ants' nests

Strong,
sharp jaws
cut margin
of leaf

African bullfrog

Caterpillar

Swallowtail
butterfly

❽ DUNG FEEDERS

Certain insects feed on the feces (dung) of herbivores such as cattle. Dung beetles use smell to detect dung and suck nutritious fluid from it. They roll dung into a ball and bury it with their eggs to provide food for newly hatched larvae.

❽

Dung beetle

❾

❹ BLOOD FEEDERS

These specialized fluid feeders have a substance in their saliva that stops blood from clotting. Female mosquitoes pierce their prey's skin, then suck up blood through special mouthparts. Vampire bats use razor-sharp teeth to bite cattle and other mammals, then lap up the blood.

❺ OMNIVORES

With a diet that includes both meat and plant foods, omnivores, such as pigs, squirrels, and orang-utans, tend to be opportunists that eat most things. Some, including raccoons and foxes, live in close proximity to humans, adding garbage and roadkill to their normal diet.

❼ HERBIVORES

Pandas, muntjacs, caterpillars, and tortoises are herbivores—animals that eat plant parts using special teeth or other mouthparts. Leaves and stems are not very nutritious, so herbivores must consume large amounts to obtain enough nutrients.

❻ FILTER FEEDERS

Most filter feeders, from small rock-bound barnacles to mighty baleen whales, live in water. They filter tiny organisms from the water around them using sievelike body parts. Flamingos, the only filter-feeding birds, eat tiny crustaceans.

Orang-utan

Bamboo forms 99 percent of this Chinese bear's diet

Giant Panda

❻ Flamingo

Muntjac

Large, flattened teeth grind up vegetation

Raccoon

Sea eagle

Snake suffocates its prey in its coils, then swallows it whole

Beak held upside down to strain food from water

Boa constrictor

❽ FLUID FEEDERS

Fluid feeders suck liquid food through tubelike mouthparts. Butterflies have a long, coiled-up proboscis that unrolls to drink energy-rich nectar from flowers. Aphids pierce plant stems using their mouthparts to suck up sugary sap.

Tortoise

Sharp talons grab fish from the water

Mosquito

MOVEMENT

One of the major things that makes animals stand out from other living things, such as plants and fungi, is their ability to move. While some stay rooted to one place and move body parts, most move about actively in the air, on land, or in water. Animals move in many different ways, from swimming to sidewinding, and looping to leaping.

❶ TIGER
Walking and running on four legs are movements performed not only by tigers and other cats, but also by many other mammals. Aside from supporting the body's weight, legs can be moved in coordinated ways by muscles under the control of the brain. The tiger's long tail helps it to balance when running or pouncing.

❷ FLAT-TAILED GECKO
These agile lizards make adept climbers, scaling vertical surfaces and even hanging upside down as they search for insect prey. They owe these skills to five wide toe pads on each foot that are covered with millions of tiny hairs. These create electrical forces that glue the gecko to any surface, even glass.

❸ LOOPER CATERPILLAR
Certain caterpillars travel with a looping movement. The caterpillar anchors itself with claspers at its rear end, and reaches forward with its front end. When it has fixed its front end in place using its legs, it pulls its back end forward to form a loop. It then repeats the sequence to continue moving forward.

❹ SIDEWINDING SNAKE
Most snakes move by wriggling from side to side to form S-shaped curves that push the body forward. In the desert, snakes have to move over hot sand. Some do this by sidewinding—throwing their bodies in sideways leaps so that they move diagonally and touch the hot ground as little as possible—leaving a trail of markings where they have landed.

❺ COMMON FROG
At home both on land and in water, frogs use different methods of movement for each environment. Frogs can walk, but they also leap, especially to escape enemies. Powerful hind legs push the body off the ground and shorter forelegs absorb the shock of landing. In water, the webbed hind feet kick out to propel the frog forward.

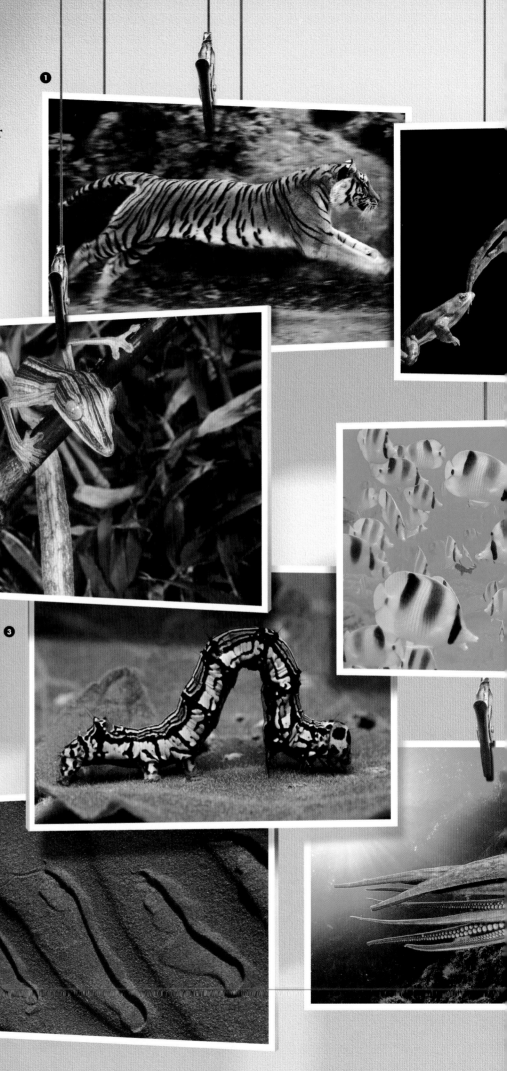

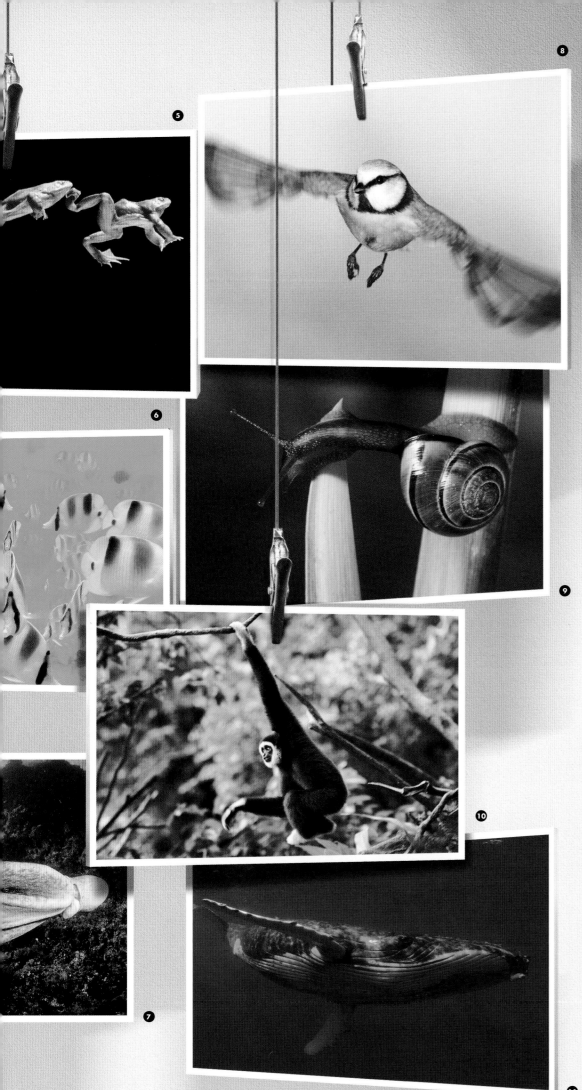

❻ FISH

On both sides of a fish's backbone there are muscles that contract (pull) to move the tail from side to side and push the fish forward. Fins also stabilize the fish's body, preventing it from tipping from side to side or up and down, and enable it to steer.

❼ OCTOPUS

The octopus uses its long tentacles and suckers to pull itself over the seafloor, but it can also swim rapidly, just as squid and cuttlefish do. It takes water into its body then expels it through a funnel-like siphon. This creates a jet of water that propels the octopus through the ocean, head first and with tentacles trailing.

❽ BLUE TIT

Most birds use their wings to fly. When the wings are pulled downward and backward, they push the bird forward. This forces air over the curved surfaces of the wings, creating the lift that keeps the bird airborne. Body feathers give this blue tit a streamlined shape, while the tail acts as a rudder.

❾ SNAIL

Slugs and snails have a single, large foot on which they creep across the ground or along plants. Muscles in the underside of the foot contract and relax to create wavelike ripples that push the snail slowly forward. The foot also produces slippery slime that makes creeping easier and protects the snail from any sharp objects in its path.

❿ GIBBON

Found in the tropical rain forests of southeast Asia, gibbons are apes with long arms and very flexible shoulder and wrist joints. These features enable them to perform an action called brachiation. Gibbons hurl themselves forward, swinging hand over hand from branch to branch to move with great speed and skill through the forest canopy.

⓫ HUMPBACK WHALE

This massive marine mammal swims using its tail. The tail fin has two horizontal paddles called flukes, which can be moved up and down by muscle action to propel the whale forward, downward, or upward to the surface to breathe air. Its broad front limbs or flippers steer the whale so it can turn.

SPEED

The members of the animal kingdom move at widely differing speeds. How fast an animal can move depends on many factors, including its size, shape, and weight, whether it lives in the air, on land, or in water, and the way it moves. In general, larger animals move fastest, especially those that live in open habitats such as grasslands or the ocean. Here are the slowest, the fastest, and some in between.

0.03 mph
(0.05 kph)

6 mph
(10 kph)

22 mph
(35 kph)

25 mph
(40 kph)

3 mph
(5 kph)

33 mph
(53 kph)

GARDEN SNAIL
Making leisurely progress on a film of slimy mucus, the garden snail is not built for speed. It creeps forward as a result of waves of contractions rippling down its single, muscular foot. If threatened the snail cannot flee, but retreats inside its protective shell.

BUMBLEBEE
Despite their apparent bulkiness, these flower-feeding insects can use their wings to reach a good flying speed. On cool days, they beat their wings to warm up their bodies before taking off.

GENTOO PENGUIN
With sleek, streamlined bodies, penguins move with ease in the ocean, powered by their flipperlike wings. The fastest, South Atlantic gentoo penguins, dart and turn to catch krill and fish, and to escape enemies.

BLACK RHINOCEROS
This heavily built, powerful African mammal browses on shrubs and low trees and has no natural enemies, aside from humans. Nonetheless, black rhinos have poor eyesight and will charge with speed and agility if spooked by strange smells or sounds.

COCKROACH
The fastest running insect, an American cockroach uses long legs to dart out of sight. It can conceal itself in the narrowest crevice.

TIGER SHARK
The ferocious tiger shark eats anything, including jellyfish, seals, turtles, dolphins, and even humans. It lives in warm coastal waters, where it uses rapid bursts of speed to catch its often fast-moving prey. It has a streamlined shape and powerful muscles that pull its tail from side to side.

SAILFISH
Powered by mighty muscles and a crescent-shaped tail, the sailfish is the fastest fish in the warmer oceans. Its sail-like dorsal fin is normally folded down, but raises to help the sailfish herd its prey, such as sardines, making them easier to catch.

70 mph
(110 kph)

55 mph
(88 kph)

PRONGHORN
One of the quickest land mammals, the North American pronghorn is related to deer and antelope. The pronghorn lives in scrub and open grassland and uses its long legs to move quickly over long distances.

175 mph
(280 kph)

60 mph
(100 kph)

45 mph
(72 kph)

PEREGRINE FALCON
This bird-hunting predator is the fastest animal on the planet. The peregrine falcon soars to a great height and then, with wings partially folded, dives at breathtaking speed on prey flying far below it. With a well-aimed slash of its talons, the peregrine knocks the prey to the ground, ready to be eaten.

OSTRICH
The world's biggest bird may not fly, but it can run faster than any other bird. In the African savanna, ostriches sustain high speeds over long distances as they seek food or escape predators, such as lions. Ostriches have long legs powered by massive muscles. These not only propel them at speed but can also deliver a deadly kick to enemies.

CHEETAH
Over short distances this daytime hunter is the fastest land animal. It pursues its prey with an explosive burst of speed, but if a kill is not made within 30 seconds, the cheetah stops to keep from overheating.

MAINTENANCE

The animal world is a tough, competitive place, and animals have to look after themselves and keep in peak condition in order to increase their chances of survival. Animals maintain themselves for many reasons: to enable them to move more efficiently, to help them attract a mate so they can breed, to remove pesky parasites, and to stay healthy. Maintenance methods include grooming, preening, eating special foods, and taking mud baths.

❶ SOCIAL GROOMING

Many primates, such as these Japanese macaques, live in tight-knit groups. Group members groom each other, using their nails and teeth to comb and clean each other's fur, and to remove any irritating parasites, such as lice.

❷ INSECT CLEAN-UP

Dust and food particles can cling to an insect's body parts and stop them from working well. Insects use their legs and mouthparts to clean themselves. This praying mantis is grooming the spines on its front legs.

❸ SELF-GROOMING

Cats and some other mammals groom themselves. A tiger, for example, uses its rough, moist tongue to clean its fur and remove pests. Kangaroos spread saliva on themselves, which then evaporates to give a cooling effect.

❹ CLAY LICK

A number of animals living in tropical forests, both birds and mammals, eat small amounts of clay each day. Flocks of colorful, squawking parrots descend on favoured spots, called clay licks. It appears that the clay makes harmless any poisons in the fruits, nuts, and seeds that the parrots eat.

❶ Macaque grooms another group member

❸ Parrot eats mineral-rich clay obtained from a clay lick

❹

A moistened paw can reach other parts of the tiger's body

❷ Prey-gripping spines on front legs must be kept clean

❺ Coating of mud keeps the hippo's skin cool and moist

❺ MUD BATH

Hippopotamuses depend on mud baths or water to keep themselves cool in the African heat. The water or mud also protects their sensitive skin from the bites of insects and other pests. If not regularly moistened, their skin dries out very easily, and can crack and become infected.

❻ SHOWERING

In the hot African savanna, elephants visit waterholes to drink and cool off. They use their trunks to suck up water, then squirt it into their mouths, or point it backward to shower cooling water over their thick skin. Wet skin traps a layer of dust that protects against parasites and sunlight.

❼ PREENING FEATHERS

To ensure flying is as efficent as possible, birds use their beaks to preen their feathers. The tip of the beak works like a comb to straighten and clean feathers. Preening also spreads an oily liquid over the feathers to waterproof them, and roots out any parasites living on the skin.

❽ BIRD ANTING

Eurasian jays are among the birds that use this type of maintenance. The bird lies on top of an ants' nest, provoking the irritated ants to spray chemicals, such as formic acid, onto its feathers. These chemicals kill irritating, blood-feeding parasites.

Flight feathers spread out for preening

Tail fanned out over ants' nest

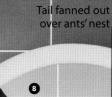

SENSES

An animal's senses provide a constant stream of information about its surroundings, using receptors that send signals to the brain. This enables the animal to avoid danger, find food, locate a mate, navigate, and communicate. The main five senses are sight, hearing, smell, taste, and touch. Sharks are ocean predators. As well as the main five, sharks have two extra senses that enhance their hunting efficiency.

Lateral line runs along the length of the shark's body

❶ TOUCH

Most animals, including sharks, have touch receptors scattered throughout the skin. Receptors for other senses are usually found in special organs, such as the eyes. The shark's touch receptors detect water currents, temperature changes, and direct contact with other animals, especially when a shark goes in for the kill.

❷ VIBRATIONS

A fluid-filled tube called the lateral line runs along the length of the shark from head to tail. Pores in the skin connect the surrounding water to lateral-line receptors that detect vibrations and pressure changes. This provides the shark with a sense of "distant touch" that allows it to sense the intensity and direction of the movements of an approaching fish.

❸ HEARING AND BALANCE

Two small openings in the top of the shark's head mark the entrance to the inner parts of a shark's ears. Sounds travel farther and faster in water than in air, and sharks are able to pinpoint prey over several miles by detecting the low frequency sounds they produce. As in many other animals, balance organs in the shark's ears help it stay orientated and upright.

❷

Position of lateral line as it extends toward tail

❹ SIGHT

A shark's large, well-developed eyes are more sensitive than human eyes. With increasing depths, light levels in the ocean decrease and the eye's pupils widen to admit more light. In addition, a layer called the tapetum lucidum lining the shark's eyes reflects light internally, maximizing the shark's vision so it can hunt in the darkness.

❺ TASTE

Sharks do not use their sense of taste to detect their prey, but to determine whether they want to eat it or not. Pits in the mouth and throat contain receptors called taste buds. As the shark bites, the taste buds detect chemicals in its prey's tissues. If the shark finds the animal "tasty," perhaps because it contains plenty of fat, it will continue eating.

Openings to ears located on top of head just behind the eyes

Eye rolls backward during feeding for protection

Pores mark openings to organs that detect electrical signals

Water passing through nostrils carries odors to smell receptors

Taste buds located in lining of mouth and gullet

❻ SMELL

As a shark swims, water flows into its nostrils and over highly sensitive smell receptors. Once the shark picks up on an odor trail, it swims toward the source, moving its head from side to side to pinpoint the exact location.

❼ ELECTRICAL SIGNALS

When animals move, their muscles give off very weak electrical signals. Dotted around the shark's snout are hundreds of pores leading to sensory organs that can detect those electrical signals. Once a shark has seen, heard, or smelled its prey and is closing in, its electrical detectors take over, using the prey's weak electrical signals to strike accurately.

Skin contains touch, temperature, and pain receptors

Wolf spider eyes are arranged in rows and allow for effective night-time hunting

VISION

For many animals, vision is their most important sense. They use it to create an image of their surroundings so that they can navigate, find food and mates, avoid predators, and communicate with each other. Animals can see because they have light receptors, usually housed inside special sense organs called eyes. These receptors turn light into nerve signals, which are then turned back into images by the brain. Quality of vision varies greatly between different species. Flatworms can distinguish only between light and dark, while some mammal eyes generate 3-D color images.

▲ SPIDER EYES

All spiders have eight simple eyes, but many depend more on their sense of touch to detect and trap their prey. However, active hunters, such as jumping spiders and this wolf spider, use large, forward-facing eyes to locate and catch prey.

▲ CEPHALOPOD EYES

Octopuses and other cephalopod mollusks have highly developed eyes. They allow their owners to find and catch prey, and to navigate away from predators. Unlike other cephalopods, cuttlefish have unusual W-shaped pupils.

▲ FORWARD-FACING EYES

Forward-facing eyes enable hunters, like this eagle, to judge distances accurately so they can pounce on moving prey. Tree-dwelling primates, such as monkeys, also have forward-facing eyes, which allow them to jump safely from branch to branch.

▲ EYESPOTS

The most simple eyes are eyespots. In water-dwelling flatworms, cup-shaped eyespots act as simple light detectors, enabling the flatworm to shy away from bright light and move to darker, safer areas under rocks or plants.

▲ NIGHT VISION

Like many nocturnal animals, red-eyed tree frogs have large eyes in relation to their overall body size that are efficient at capturing light in dim conditions. In the tropical forests of South America, they use their keen night vision to ambush moths, flies, and crickets.

Thick eyelashes
protect eye from
dirt and insects

▲ EYES ON STALKS
Like many crabs, shore-dwelling ghost crabs have compound eyes on stalks, giving them an all-around view of their surroundings. If they spot danger, they disappear instantly into their burrows. The stalked eyes can also be folded down for protection.

▲ ALL-AROUND VISION
Animals—such as rabbits, antelopes, and deer—that graze or browse on vegetation, have large eyes on the sides of their heads that allow them to see to the front, sideways, and behind. This all-around vision allows them to keep a constant lookout for predators.

▲ INDEPENDENT EYES
A chameleon swivels its two eyes independently of one another as it looks out for insects. Once prey is sighted, both eyes swivel forward so the lizard can judge the distance accurately as it shoots out a long, sticky tongue to grab its victim.

▲ COMPOUND EYES
Crustaceans, such as crabs, and insects, including this dragonfly, have compound eyes made up of lots of separate light-detection units, each with its own lens for focusing light. The animal's brain receives signals from all these units to produce a "mosaic" image.

▲ MIRROR EYES
A scallop, like a mussel, is a mollusk that has two hinged shells enclosing its body. When the shells open, they expose two rows of small eyes. Inside each eye, a mirrorlike surface reflects light onto receptors to form images.

▲ ABOVE AND BELOW
The four-eyed fish floats on the surface of fresh water. It has two eyes, each divided into two parts. The upper half of each eye is adapted for vision in air, so it can see insect prey on the water's surface. The lower half sees underwater.

▲ WIDELY SEPARATED EYES
The hammerhead shark has eyes located at the tips of extensions on each side of its head. Being widely separated, they give the hammerhead a much bigger visual range than other sharks as it swims along in search of prey.

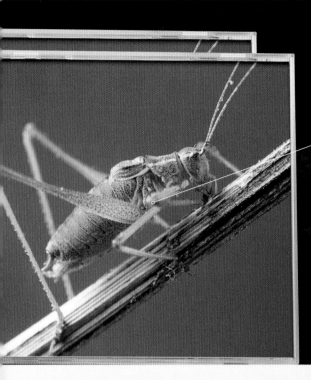

Eardrum just below knee of front leg

BAT ▶
Finding food at night is not a problem for insect-eating bats. They produce high-pitched sounds that bounce off potential prey, such as moths. Their highly sensitive ears detect these echoes and the bat then uses them to pinpoint the position of its prey.

◀ CRICKET
A keen sense of hearing enables crickets to hear the chirping sounds produced by potential mates or rivals. Sounds are picked up by a thin membrane located on the cricket's knee.

Large ears open wide to capture sounds

◀ AFRICAN ELEPHANT
Elephants communicate using sounds that humans can hear. But they also produce very low-pitched sounds that travel over long distances to keep the herd in touch. African elephants pick up these sounds with their ears, and from the ground through their feet and trunks.

SERVAL ▼
An African savanna cat, the serval has long legs that allow it to see over tall grasses and large ear flaps that move to pick up even the faintest sounds made by small prey, especially rodents. Once the prey's position is pinpointed, the serval leaps and pounces.

Large, movable ears detect prey

HEARING

Whether it is used to find food, recognize mates, pick up sounds made by rivals, or detect the approach of a hungry predator, hearing is a vitally important sense for many animals. Sound waves travel through air or water from a vibrating source, such as an elephant's vocal cords or a cricket's wings. Many animals pick up sound waves using a membrane called the eardrum that is linked to sound receptors within the ear.

◄ DOLPHIN

Although dolphins have excellent eyesight, these marine mammals also use echolocation to find food. They produce bursts of high-pitched clicks that are beamed in front of the dolphin, focused by a lump of fatty tissue called the melon. Sounds bounce off objects and their echoes are channeled via the lower jaw to the ears. The dolphin can then analyze the echoes to pinpoint prey.

Bulge contains fat-filled melon

BARN OWL ▼

This nocturnal hunter uses its acute sense of hearing to detect rustling sounds made by potential prey. A ruff of feathers channels sounds into the ear openings, which are asymmetrical to pinpoint prey accurately.

Right ear opening is higher than the left one

◄ BULLFROG

Hearing is a very important sense in amphibians. It enables them to identify and pinpoint calls made by mates and potential rivals, and to detect predators. Bullfrogs have no external ears but pick up sounds through large eardrums on the sides of the head.

Eardrum is just behind the eye

◄ KANGAROO RAT

As it hops across American deserts at night, a kangaroo rat listens for danger. Its ears can amplify (make louder) sounds by 100 times, so it can detect a rustling rattlesnake, its main predator.

SMELL AND TASTE

The ability to smell and taste varies enormously throughout the animal kingdom. An animal with a sense of smell has detectors that pick up odor molecules from objects, enabling it to find food or mates, identify other members of its species, detect predators, or find its way home. A sense of taste involves direct contact with food in order to test if it is a tasty meal that is safe to eat.

❶ AFRICAN WILD DOG

African wild dogs, like other members of the dog family, are predators with a powerful sense of smell. Dogs use smell to track prey over long distances, to identify other members of the pack, and to pick up scents left by outsiders marking their territory.

❷ FRUIT BAT

While insect-eating bats depend on their acute sense of hearing to detect prey, larger fruit-eating bats use their excellent senses of smell and vision to find food. Also called flying foxes, they live in tropical areas where there is a constant supply of fruit. Some species of fruit bat feed on flowers, nectar, and pollen, also found in tropical areas.

❸ KIWI

Native to New Zealand, this nocturnal, flightless bird has poor sight, but, unlike most birds, it has a great sense of smell. The kiwi has two nostrils at the tip of its long beak. As it looks for food, the kiwi pushes its beak into the soil to sniff out worms, beetle larvae, centipedes, and other juicy food items.

❹ TAPIR

A tapir lifts its upper lip to expose the opening of its Jacobson's organ, located in the roof of the mouth, which enhances the ability to smell and taste. This action, called a flehmen response, draws in airborne scents. It is also performed by lions and some other mammals, and is used mainly to pick up smells given off by potential mates.

❺ MOTH

Insects use the two antennae attached to their heads to detect smells and tastes, as well as to touch. Some male moths have feathery antennae that are supersensitive to pheromones (chemical signals) released by females, often hundreds of yards away. As they fly at night, males pick up the scent trail and follow it to find a potential mate.

❻ MONKEY

Japanese macaques, like other monkeys, use their excellent sense of vision to spot fruit. Their senses of smell and taste then take over. As the macaque bites into a fruit, smell detectors in its nose pick up odors from the flesh, and taste buds on its tongue detect tastes, such as sweetness. A bitter taste warns that the fruit may be poisonous and should be discarded.

❼ OCTOPUS

These intelligent mollusks hunt mainly at night for fish, crabs, and other prey. An octopus's eight flexible, muscular arms reach out to move and to grasp food. Each arm is equipped with numerous suckers that grip the seabed and hold onto prey. The suckers also taste prey to see if it is worth eating.

❽ SNAKE

Like a tapir, a snake has a Jacobson's organ housed in the roof of its mouth, which detects both tastes and smells. By flicking out its tongue, the snake collects odor molecules. These are identified when the tongue is pressed against the Jacobson's organ. Snakes use this combined sense to locate food and potential mates.

❾ TURKEY VULTURE

While other vultures use sight to find the dead animals on which they feed, turkey vultures employ a different strategy. Found in North and South America, the turkey vulture uses its sense of smell. As it soars and glides, the vulture can pick up odors given off by rotting corpses on the ground, even if they are hidden in dense forest.

❿ CATFISH

Named for the whiskerlike barbels around their mouths, catfish have poor vision and live in the murky depths of lakes and rivers. Their long barbels are equipped with lots of taste sensors. As the catfish's snout probes the lake or riverbed, the barbels feel for food and taste it to determine whether it is edible.

COMMUNICATION

Animals communicate with each other in a huge number of different ways. They make sounds, release odors, use touch, gestures, and body language, and even produce flashing lights. Communication is an important tool for attracting a mate, holding a social group together, marking a territory, or alerting other group members to a food source, rival, or an approaching predator.

❶ CHIMPANZEE
Like many other animals, chimps use gestures and body language to communicate with other members of their social group. But these intelligent primates also use facial expressions to show anger, fear, happiness, playfulness, and hunger, and to indicate their status in the group.

Grimace made when higher-ranking chimp approaches

Stripy tail used for visual signaling

❷ FIREFLY

These night-flying beetles use light to communicate with each other. An organ in the firefly's abdomen produces flashes of light that it uses to attract mates. Some female fireflies imitate the light flashes of other species to lure male fireflies, which they then eat.

❸ RING-TAILED LEMUR

Relatives of monkeys, lemurs depend heavily on their sense of smell for communication. Male ring-tailed lemurs use a scent gland in their wrist to mark their territory. They also have stink fights against rivals—rubbing their tails against their scent glands and waving them in the air as "smelly flags."

❹ HONEYBEE

When foraging worker honeybees return to the hive, they perform "dances" to tell other workers the direction and distance of good sources of nectar and pollen. The other bees use their antennae to detect the smell of nectar and to track the movements of the newly returned worker through touch.

❻ ANT

When ants from the same colony meet they smell each other using their antennae. In this way, they can detect whether or not they belong to the same group, and if one has discovered a good food source that others can exploit. Such communication allows ants to function as complex societies.

❺ GANNET

Many male and female birds use body language during courtship and, if they stay together for a long time, to reinforce the bond between them. Gannets perform special greeting ceremonies, stretching their necks and beaks skyward and gently tapping or rubbing their beaks together.

❼ TREE FROG

Communicating by sound can be risky, because it may attract predators. Yet many male frogs, including tree frogs, make a loud, croaky call to attract females or deter rivals. Sounds are produced by the vocal cords and amplified when air is forced into the bulging vocal sac.

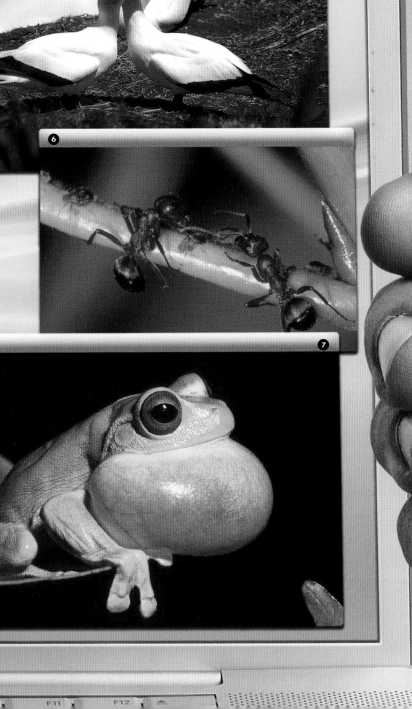

IP 82.184

❽ WOLF

Although they live in packs, wolves often get separated when they go hunting. To maintain contact and identify themselves, they howl. Howling sounds travel over long distances and bring the pack back together.

DEFENSES

For many animals there is a near-constant threat of attack by predators in search of food. Those with keen senses and quick reactions can make a dash for safety and hide themselves. Others employ a wide range of strategies—including armor, chemical warfare, or even pretending to be dead—to defend themselves against hungry attackers.

❶ LOOKING BIGGER

With fur raised and back arched, a cat makes itself appear bigger to frighten off an enemy. Many animals use the same method. The Australian frilled lizard expands its neck collar, opens its mouth, and waves its tail to look bigger and more scary.

❷ ARMOR

Many insects, crustaceans, and some mammals, such as armadillos, have a hard outer covering that provides a degree of protection from hungry predators. Certain types of woodlice, called pill bugs, have jointed armor and can roll into a ball to protect their softer underparts.

❸ SPINES

Sharp spines provide a very effective deterrent, as any porcupine illustrates. Inhabitants of rocky shores and reefs, black sea urchins are armed with movable spines that put off all but the most determined of predators. The spines also inject poison if they penetrate the skin.

❹ CHEMICAL ATTACK

Many animals, especially insects, contain poisonous or irritating chemicals that make them inedible. Some launch a more direct attack. The bombardier beetle bends its abdomen forward and squirts out a cocktail of chemicals that distracts, burns, and may even blind its enemy.

❺ SAFETY IN NUMBERS

Living as a group—be it a shoal of fish, a herd of wildebeest, or this flock of snow geese—has great defense benefits. It is more difficult for a predator to pick off individuals from a moving group, and members can warn others of approaching danger.

❻ SMOKESCREEN

A threatened octopus squirts a billowing cloud of brown ink into the water around it. While the confused predator attacks the cloud, the octopus is able to make a jet-propelled escape. Squid use the same means of defense.

❼ SCARE TACTICS

Many butterflies and moths have patterned spots on their upper wing surfaces that resemble large eyes. When this owl butterfly opens its wings, a predator sees the "eyes" and backs off, thinking its potential prey is big and fierce.

❽ PLAYING DEAD

Many predators are only attracted to moving prey, so they lose interest if their target plays dead. By lying still with its mouth open, this grass snake appears to have died, but it will soon come back to life once its attacker has moved on.

❾ LOSING BODY PARTS

As a dramatic defense ploy, a threatened blue-tailed skink sheds the tip of its tail. The lost tip continues to wiggle for a while, distracting the predator while the lizard makes its escape. Amazingly, the tail grows back over the following weeks and months.

Lizard expands collar of skin in order to appear bigger

⑩ HIDING

What could be simpler than running away and hiding when an enemy appears? A burrow provides a safe haven for these ground squirrels. They feed near the entrance so they can make a rapid escape when trouble threatens.

7

8

Eyes appear suddenly when butterfly opens its wings

Gaping mouth makes the snake appear dead

5

9

Blood vessels close up at the fracture point to reduce bleeding

10

Cloud of ink left by octopus as it escapes

6

❶ NATURAL MATCH

Many animals naturally merge into their habitat. The tan color of a lion is a perfect match for the tall savanna grasses that conceal it as it stalks prey. The wings of the willow beauty moth match the color and texture of a tree trunk, making it all but invisible to birds that prey on it.

❷ SEASONAL CHANGE

Arctic regions have short summers and long, snowy winters. Some animals change color seasonally to maintain their camouflage all year round. In the fall, the ptarmigan's brown plumage turns white, making it less visible in the snow. In spring it turns brown again.

❸ RAPID COLOR CHANGE

An octopus can change the color and pattern of its body within seconds to match its surroundings by either shrinking or expanding packets of pigment (coloring) in its skin. The chameleon is another rapid changer, although it also alters its colors in order to communicate.

❹ DECORATION

Some animals adorn themselves with objects from their surroundings to conceal their identity. The decorator crab attaches pieces of seaweed, pebbles, shells, and even corals and sponges, to blend in with the seabed. This camouflage covering is held in place by tiny hooks on the crab's shell.

Decorator crab

Sponge attached to crab

Camouflaged octopus matches stony seabed

Octopus

Chameleon

Plumage matches pebbles and rocks

Ptarmigan in summer

Ptarmigan in winter

Fur and eye colorings match grasses

Lion

Willow beauty moth

76

➎ DISRUPTIVE COLORATION

Distinctive patterns and bright colors are sometimes used as warnings that highlight an animal's presence, but in some species they actually serve to break up the animal's body outline and make it difficult to see. A tiger's stripes make it almost invisible to prey as it moves through long grasses. Brightly patterned reef fish are difficult targets for stalking predators.

➏ MASQUERADE

Masquerading as part of their surroundings or as something inedible is a strategy used by certain animals to conceal themselves. Stick insects mimic the twigs among which they live. The caterpillar of the giant swallowtail butterfly looks like a bird dropping—a deterrent for most predators. At rest with its wings folded, a lappet moth resembles dead leaves.

➐ COUNTERSHADING

Penguins use countershading to make them less obvious. Seen from above, a penguin's dark back merges into the deep, murky water below. Seen from below, its pale belly matches the light penetrating the sea's surface. The okapi uses countershading to conceal it in the dense forests where it lives.

➎ Tiger prowls unnoticed

Stick insect sways to mimic twigs blowing in the wind

Tiger

Butterfish

Colors confuse predators

➏ Stick insect

Swallowtail butterfly caterpillar

Lappet moth

Brown back blends in with shadowy forest

Part of body exposed to light is dark

➐

Okapi

Penguin

Part of body normally in shadow is light

Striped legs help hide the okapi between the forest trees

CAMOUFLAGE

A predator has a much greater chance of catching prey if it cannot easily be seen, while its victim is less likely to be caught and eaten if it blends into its surroundings. Some animals have natural camouflage that makes them less visible. Body color, stripes and patterns, or even looking like something inedible can provide a life-saving cloak of invisibility.

WARNINGS

Rather than hiding themselves, or having elaborate defenses, some animals give clear warnings to predators or competitors either to stay away or risk getting hurt. Warnings can take the form of sounds, gestures, or bright colors, which announce that an animal is dangerous, poisonous, or both. A few animals even mimic the colors or shapes of other poisonous animals in order to trick enemies into believing that they are dangerous.

❷ POISON DART FROG

These small, brightly colored frogs from Central and South America release poison from glands in their skin that can kill predators, such as snakes and spiders. Their bright colors and patterns advertise the fact that they are not good to eat.

❸ LION

Big cats roar to warn others to stay out of their territory. In addition to the loud sound, an open mouth displays the lion's sharp teeth and makes its head looks bigger and scarier. Other animals that display their teeth include monkeys.

❶ RATTLESNAKE

These highly venomous snakes have a warning rattle at the end of their tail. If threatened by a predator or a large animal that might step on it, the rattlesnake vibrates its rattle, producing a loud buzz.

Rattle is made from modified scales

Wide open mouth shows off the lion's sharp teeth

Bright colors mark the frog as being poisonous

Bright red stripes are a sign of danger

❹ BLISTER BEETLE

Its red and black coloration identifies the blister beetle as an animal to be avoided. If attacked, it releases a poisonous chemical that causes blistering and deters would-be predators from disturbing the beetle again.

❺ WASP AND HOVERFLY

The yellow and black colors of a common wasp provide a warning to predators that it has a powerful sting. The unrelated hoverfly mimics the wasp's stripey appearance, thereby deterring predators even though it is harmless.

❻ SKUNK

Even a predator as big as a bear can get into trouble if it ignores a skunk's warning colors. After hissing and foot-stamping, the skunk sprays its attacker with a stinking fluid that can irritate or even cause blindness.

❼ VENOMOUS FISH

The colored stripes of the zebra lionfish send out a clear message to potential predators that its long spines are highly poisonous. If threatened, the fish puts its head down so the spines point forward, ready for action.

❽ SCARY CATERPILLARS

Being vulnerable to bird predators, some caterpillars attempt to scare them away. The puss moth caterpillar raises its facelike head, waves its tails, and may squirt acid. The hawkmoth caterpillar mimics a poisonous snake.

❾ BUTTERFLY MARKINGS

Birds that try to eat the foul-tasting monarch butterfly do not repeat the experience and remember the patterns of their wings for the future. The viceroy butterfly has a similar appearance, and also tastes horrible.

Hoverfly's markings mimic those of the wasp

Black and white warning colors

"Tails" are lifted and waved when caterpillar is threatened

Wasp has clear yellow and black stripes

Long spines filled with venom

Head raised to reveal a colorful but false face

Puss moth caterpillar

Hawkmoth caterpillar

Startling eyespots mimic a snake's eyes

Viceroy butterfly

Monarch butterfly

COMPETITION

Animals are constantly competing for access to vitally important but limited resources, such as food, mates, and territory. Competition happens between individuals of the same species, but may also occur between different species. Some animals attempt to assert their dominance and deter rivals through a threat display or a ritualized fight—a strategy that prevents harm to either side. But sometimes competition involves real fights in which one or both animals may suffer injury.

❶ NECK WRESTLING

Male giraffes engage in ritualized fights known as necking. Two males stand with their necks entwined and then push from side to side. Necking establishes which are the strongest males. These are the only ones that will mate with females.

❷ STANDOFF

If an animal can avoid injury in a fight by deterring a rival, so much the better. In standoffs between some mammals, the open mouth is a common threat display. By "yawning," this hippopotamus bares its enormous mouth and teeth.

Male giraffes push with their long necks

Wide open mouth warns off enemies and rivals

Bighorn sheep's thick skull absorbs the head-on impact

Strong jaws used to lift rival during a fight

❸ BETWEEN SPECIES

In the African savanna, when an animal dies or is killed, vultures crowd around the remains, fighting among themselves for scraps. When scavenging hyenas arrive, the vultures scatter, returning to the carcass to feed warily in the presence of these powerful carnivores.

❹ STAG BEETLES

With their massive jaws it might appear that male stag beetles catch large prey. In fact, they feed on tree sap and use their jaws to fight other males for mates and favored mating sites. The winning male lifts an opponent and turns him onto his back. The loser then retreats uninjured.

❺ HEAD ON

At the start of their breeding season in the fall, male bighorn sheep have head-butting contests. Two males run at each other, ramming their heads together. This can go on for hours until one male gives up. The overall "winner" within the herd mates with the most females.

❻ DECLARING TERRITORY

Songbirds do not sing to give us pleasure but to tell other members of their species to keep out of their territory. European robins, for example, defend the territory that supplies them and their offspring with food. Persistent intruders are attacked and driven out.

❼ WARNING CALL

In the fall, male red deer round up females to prevent them from mating with other males. They roar at their rivals, the loudness of their bellowing indicating their fighting ability. Roaring alone may ensure a stag's success, but if not, he locks antlers with rivals and fights.

❽ ON THE BEACH

During their breeding season, male elephant seals strive to command the largest territory and the most females. Initially, a male makes booming noises to intimidate rivals. If that fails, the enormous creatures fight on the beach, inflicting wounds until one retreats.

Antlers used for fighting

Competing male seals bite and push against each other

❼

❺

❻

❾ LIZARD THREAT

Many lizards change color or perform some other display when their territory is threatened. A male green anole flicks down its pink dewlap (throat fan) to warn off intruders. It emphasizes the message by bobbing its head up and down.

❾

Beak opens wide as the European robin sings to defend its territory

Pink dewlap exposed as a threat

❽

INSTINCT

Everything an animal does—and the way in which it does it—makes up its behavior. Some behaviors are learned during an animal's lifetime, but many are inbuilt or instinctive. They are performed automatically in situations such as courtship, breeding, or nest building.

1.

Free-floating silk dragline catches twig

Spider anchors line of silk and pulls it tight

Vertical thread pulled downward to create "Y" scaffold

Spider trails out second horizontal thread

2.

Additional threads frame the "Y" scaffold

3.

4.

WEB SPINNING ▼

Spiders have special glands for producing strong silk threads. Orb web spiders use silk to build spiral webs that catch flying insects. After constructing a "scaffold" of dry threads, the spider spins a spiral of sticky, insect-trapping threads. Spiders do not learn to do this. They can build the most complex of webs by instinct, even when they have just hatched.

Spoke threads travel from outside to the center of the web

Spider lays down a spiral of sticky threads

5.

◀ TURTLES

Female turtles instinctively emerge from the sea to lay their eggs, so that their offspring will breathe air when they hatch. The eggs are laid in a hole dug in the sand, which is then covered up. A few weeks later, the eggs hatch. The hatchling turtles automatically dig upward, then dash straight toward the open sea.

Finished web now ready to trap insects

◄ LEAPING SALMON

After hatching in streams and rivers, then migrating out to sea for years of feeding, salmon instinctively return to where they came from in order to breed. So strong is the drive to breed that salmon will leap up and over rapids and waterfalls to reach their destination.

▲ BIRDS NESTING

Most species of birds, such as these black-headed weavers, know instinctively how to build the nests in which they incubate eggs and feed their young. In the case of weavers, male birds weave the nests and use them as a way of attracting females.

▲ DIGGER WASP

A female digger wasp uses built-in behaviors to excavate a nest hole in the ground and provide its young with food. The wasp stings and paralyzes a caterpillar, drags it into the nest, and lays her eggs in it. When they hatch, her offspring feed on the still-living prey.

CICADA CYCLE ▶

Nymphs (juvenile stages) of the periodical cicada spend 17 years feeding underground. Then they emerge above ground in their millions, become adult, mate, and die. Their offspring burrow into the soil, where they remain for the next 17 years.

LEARNING

Animals learn to change their behavior as a result of experiences, thereby increasing their chances of survival. Learning is more common in birds and mammals that have a period in their life when they are looked after by their parents, although learning can continue throughout life. Learning is often achieved through copying or by trial and error, when animals alter their behavior according to their successes and failures.

Stick provides a handy tool to extract ants from a nest

Young cheetah practises its hunting skills on a baby antelope

Young duckling soon learns to follow its mother

❶ CHEETAH
The skills needed to hunt and kill prey must be learned by young predators such as cheetahs so that as adults they can get enough food to survive. A cheetah learns by watching its mother, who provides her offspring with live prey, so they can learn by trial and error the right ways to catch and kill it.

❷ DUCKLING
Soon after they hatch, ground-nesting birds such as ducks and geese show a type of learning called imprinting. They learn to identify their mother, following and staying close to her for protection and to find food. Imprinting lasts for the first weeks of life and improves the young birds' chances of survival.

Oystercatcher teaches its young how to collect food

❸ CHIMPANZEE
Like humans, chimpanzees show insight learning—the ability to solve new problems by "putting two and two together." A chimpanzee unable to get tasty ants from a nest will figure out that if it probes the nest with a stick it can pull out a mouthful of ants. This skill will then be copied by other chimps.

❹ OYSTERCATCHER
Eurasian oystercatchers are shorebirds that probe soft sand or mud with their long, strong beaks, then use them to prize open cockles and other shelled mollusks, or to pull out marine worms. Young oystercatchers learn how to feed by watching and copying their parents.

❽ ELEPHANT

These intelligent animals live in family units of related females. Over many years a young elephant learns both social and survival skills, such as where to find food and water, or which paths to follow. It is taught not just by its mother, but also by its aunts and cousins.

Females constantly touch young elephants, providing guidance and protection

❾ JAPANESE MACAQUE

When researchers left sweet potatoes on a beach for a group of these intelligent monkeys, a female took one into the sea and washed it to remove sand—a behavior never seen before. Other group members copied this learned behavior, as did their offspring, so that food washing passed from generation to generation.

Sweet potato is washed before being eaten

❺ BOWERBIRD

Some birds mimic the sounds of other birds to defend territories and attract mates. Among the most talented mimics are the bowerbirds of Australia and New Guinea. They learn other bird songs, but also copy sounds such as cell phone ring tones, chainsaws, and car alarms.

❻ FOX CUB

Play is an enormously important part of learning in many young mammals, such as fox cubs. By "going through the motions," they learn through trial and error how to fine-tune life skills such as fighting and catching food, so that they will be able to survive and compete as adults.

Butterfly feeds on nectar from brightly colored flower

❼ BUTTERFLY

When butterflies emerge from their pupae (transition stage between caterpillar and butterfly), they have an instinctive attraction to brightly colored flowers that they will feed on. Butterflies learn by trial and error which flowers provide more or sweeter nectar.

MALE AND FEMALE

All animals reproduce to create new generations of offspring that will replace them when they die. In many species, reproduction involves males and females meeting so that mating can take place. Males and females may look very similar or, as in the examples shown here, they may differ in size and color. In these species, such differences are important in attracting mates.

Female green birdwing butterfly

Inflatable throat pouch

❶ GREAT FRIGATE BIRDS
These large seabirds spend most of their lives over the ocean, snatching prey from the water's surface or stealing from other birds. During the breeding season they gather on oceanic islands where each male inflates his distinctive red throat pouch to attract a female.

❷ PROBOSCIS MONKEYS
In many primates, including Borneo's proboscis monkeys, males are bigger than females. A male proboscis monkey also has a large, pendulous nose that attracts females. The huge nose amplifies the honking noises he makes to warn other males to stay away from his females and their young.

❸ MAROON CLOWNFISH
Some fish, especially those that live on coral reefs, change sex. The maroon clownfish lives in groups of one female and several males. If the female dies, one of the males changes to a female and takes over her role in breeding. Flame angelfish live in groups of one male and several females. If the male leaves, a female becomes male to replace him.

❹ PRAYING MANTIS
Mating can be a dangerous time for male praying mantises. The females of these predatory insects are larger than their potential mates and have been known to eat the males when mating is still in progress. When the male moves onto the female's back she may grab him with her front legs and bite his head off.

❺ BIRDWING BUTTERFLIES
Named for their large size and birdlike flying, many birdwing butterflies show differences between males and females. Spotting a vividly colored male green birdwing in an Australasian tropical forest would be easier than seeing a female, which is larger but has a duller, brown coloration.

❻ GIBBONS
Crested black gibbons are found in the tropical forests of southeast Asia. They start life with pale fur, then turn black. The males remain black, but the females become light again.

Maroon clownfish

Flame angelfish

Male praying mantis mates with a female

Large, branched antlers

⑦ ECLECTUS PARROTS

Many parrots show color differences between the sexes, but few differ as dramatically as eclectus parrots. Early naturalists believed they belonged to separate species. Unusually for parrots, the female's red plumage makes her stand out when feeding among foliage.

⑧ DEER

In summer, male deer grow bony antlers. During the mating season in the fall, stags use their antlers to attract females and to fight rival males. In winter, the antler bones die and the antlers are shed.

⑨ GOLDEN ORB SPIDERS

The male golden orb web spider, as with many other spider species, is much smaller than the female and at risk of being eaten by her. The benefit of being so tiny is that the male can mate with the female, or steal her food, without being noticed.

Female deer is smaller than the male

⑧

⑥

⑦

Female eclectus parrot is crimson and blue

Female golden orb spider approached from behind by smaller male

⑨

COURTSHIP

Many male animals use courtship to attract females. The most spectacular courtship displays happen among birds. Male birds sing, dance, or use other strategies to impress potential mates. Some are brightly colored when compared to the females, and they advertise themselves using their plumage. For birds such as eagles, courtship begins a lifelong bond between partners.

KINGFISHER ▲
Courtship feeding is important for many birds, including kingfishers. The male offers food to a female to reinforce the bond between them. This may continue when she incubates the eggs so she does not go hungry.

▼ BLUE-FOOTED BOOBY
These Pacific Ocean seabirds have big, blue webbed feet. When courting, the male booby stamps his feet, lifts his tail, and then performs a strut, showing off his feet to impress a female and persuade her to mate.

LYREBIRD ▲
To attract females, the male Australian superb lyrebird fans his long, elegant tail feathers over his head. He then sings a complex song, mimicking other birds' calls as well as forest sounds, such as chainsaws.

BALD EAGLE ▼
Male and female bald eagles perform a dramatic courtship display that includes tumbling over each other in midair. They link talons and cartwheel downward through the air, separating just before they reach the ground.

◄ SAGE GROUSE

In the spring, sage grouse congregate at communal areas called leks. Male sage grouse strut around, fanning their tail feathers, and puffing out large air sacs to show off yellow neck patches and attract as many females as possible.

NIGHTJAR ▲

During the breeding season in Africa, the male standard-winged nightjar develops elongated central wing feathers. He circles a potential mate and raises these feathers vertically to impress her during dusk display flights.

BIRD OF PARADISE ▲

Male Raggiana's birds of paradise are flamboyant with long, brightly colored feathers. In the forests of New Guinea, males try to outdo their rivals by displaying their finery, including black tail wires.

CRANE ▼

Generally mating for life, cranes engage in an elaborate courtship display at the beginning of the breeding season. These Japanese cranes perform an intricate dance by bowing and leaping into the air.

BLUE PEAFOWL ▼

A native of south Asia, the male peafowl, or peacock, is brightly colored with elongated, patterned tail feathers. Female peahens, on the other hand, have drab plumage. During courtship, the peacock raises his tail feathers into a magnificent fan.

EGGS

From cockroaches to cuckoos, many different types of animals lay eggs. Inside the egg, a young animal grows and develops, nurtured by its own food supply, until it is ready to hatch. Some animals lay a few eggs and look after them. Others lay lots of eggs and leave them to develop on their own.

Leopard tortoise

Cave spider

Eggs suspended in a silk cocoon

Cockroach

Dogfish eggs

Egg purse

Pattern of cuckoo's egg resembles its host's eggs

Yolk sac feeds developing dogfish

Fish eggs

Cuckoo egg

Soft-shelled rat snake's egg

Host nest

Rat snake

Rat snake emerging from its egg

❶ TORTOISE
Found in South Africa, female leopard tortoises lay a clutch of five to thirty soft-shelled eggs under the soil. Young tortoises use a special tooth to break through the shell, before they burrow upward and emerge on the soil's surface.

❷ SPIDER
Silk is used by spiders to make a protective cocoon around their eggs. This female cave spider is suspending her bag of eggs over an overhanging ledge. After hatching, some of the spiderlings may eat each other before they can escape and go in search of food.

❸ COCKROACH
During its two-year life span, a female cockroach can lay up to 1,000 eggs. Batches of around 15 eggs are contained in tough protective capsules called egg purses. The female cockroach carries the egg purse for a period before sticking it to a concealed surface, where the eggs later hatch.

❹ CUCKOO
A female cuckoo lays her egg in the nest of another bird, where it is incubated by the unaware host bird. The newly hatched cuckoo pushes any other eggs out of the nest to make sure it gets all the food for itself.

❺ SNAKE
Most snakes lay soft-shelled eggs, which they then abandon. The developing snake feeds on the yolk, cushioned within a bag of fluid, and receives oxygen absorbed through its eggshell. When ready, the snake hatches by slashing open the shell using a special egg tooth.

❻ DOGFISH

This small shark's eggs are protected within leathery cases called mermaid's purses. Tendrils anchor the case to seaweed to prevent it from being swept away. After months of development, during which it is fed by a yolk sac, the young dogfish pushes its way out.

Damp feathers soon dry out

Pheasant chick

Hard eggshell chipped open by young bird

Pheasant egg

Peregrine falcon egg

Guillemot egg

Mockingbird egg

Platypus egg

Ladybug eggs

Indian stick insect eggs

Butterfly leaf eggs

Frogspawn

Ostrich egg

Newt eggs

❼ GROUND-NESTING BIRD

Birds that nest on the ground, such as pheasants, lay large clutches of hard-shelled eggs. They have a long incubation period. When hatched, the young are soon able to feed themselves.

❽ CLIFF-NESTING BIRD

Female guillemots lay their eggs, rather precariously, on narrow cliff ledges. However, if disturbed, the pointed egg simply rolls around in a circle instead of falling off the ledge. Unique markings on the egg help returning parents identify it among so many others.

❾ PLATYPUS

The female duck-billed platypus is one of only a few mammals that lay eggs. Having excavated a breeding burrow next to her home stream, she lays two soft-shelled eggs. She incubates the eggs for 10 days, and feeds her young with milk after they hatch.

❿ BUTTERFLY

When female butterflies lay their eggs, they attach them to the leaves of plants that their offspring will feed on when they hatch. However, when the caterpillars emerge from their eggs, they consume their nutritious empty eggshells first, before eating the leaves.

⓫ NEWT

Like those of frogs, newt eggs do not have shells and are laid in water. A female newt lays her eggs one at a time, using her feet to wrap each one in the leaves of water weeds in order to protect them, until the newt tadpoles are ready to hatch.

LIFE HISTORIES

After it hatches from an egg or is born, an animal grows and develops until it becomes a mature adult that can breed. Some young animals, including mammals, birds, and fish, bear a resemblance to their parents, and their life histories simply involve growth to adult size. In contrast, the life history of animals such as insects and amphibians involves a metamorphosis (transformation) through several distinct stages.

▼ COW

Mammals develop inside their mother's body, are born, and then feed on her milk. Cattle and horses are born well developed, getting to their feet soon after birth. They grow and develop over the following years until they, too, can breed. Other mammals, such as foxes and mice, are born blind and helpless. They need constant parental care, and change shape as they grow.

Cow stays close to her offspring

Calf is a smaller version of its parent

GOLDEN EAGLE ▼

When a golden eagle chick hatches, like many young birds, it is small and helpless. For 10 weeks it remains in or near the nest, dependent on its predator parents to feed it pieces of meat. When its wing feathers develop, the young eagle starts to fly and hunt. Once mature, males and females pair for life.

1. The newly hatched chick is covered with white, downy feathers.

2. After a few weeks the eagle chick has grown rapidly on a diet of fresh meat.

3. The young eagle is almost ready to fly. The parent ignores its offspring begging for food.

4. The eagle has reached maturity and can fly and hunt for food.

1. Tadpoles breathe through gills.

2. Front and back legs appear.

3. Body begins to look froglike and tail shrinks.

4. Adult frog has compact body shape.

▲ FROG

Amphibians, such as frogs, undergo metamorphosis between tadpole and adult stage. Tadpoles hatch from eggs laid in ponds. They feed on plants and breathe using gills. After a while the tadpole's back legs, and later its front legs, emerge. Its head and eyes become more distinct, it starts breathing air through lungs, and feeds on small animals. Finally, its tail shrinks and, fully frog-shaped, it leaves the water.

PHOTOS DELIVERED HERE

1. Butterfly egg is laid on a leaf.

2. Caterpillar uses biting mouthparts to eat plants.

3. Caterpillar turns into a pupa and remains immobile for days or weeks.

4. Adult butterfly emerges.

▲ BUTTERFLY

Most insects, including butterflies, show complete metamorphosis. This means that they pass through four distinct life stages. A female butterfly lays eggs that hatch into larvae called caterpillars. Each caterpillar feeds continuously on plants, then stops moving and forms a tough outer coat to become a pupa. Inside the pupa, body tissues are reorganized to make a butterfly, which emerges when the pupa splits open.

1. Nymph lives and hunts underwater.

2. Adult emerges.

3. Wings fill with blood and expand.

4. Adult flies in search of insect prey.

▲ DRAGONFLY

Some insects go through incomplete metamorphosis, with only three stages—egg, nymph, and adult. Dragonfly eggs hatch into wingless versions of adults called nymphs. As the nymph grows it molts (sheds and regrows its outer covering, or cuticle). Then the cuticle splits open and a winged adult emerges.

1. Egg laid in bed of stream.

2. Hatchling emerges from egg.

3. Young salmon migrates to sea.

4. Mature salmon in breeding colors.

▲ SALMON

Salmon spawn (lay eggs) in freshwater streams and rivers. After the eggs hatch, the young fish feed and grow in their native waters for months or years before migrating to the sea. Here they remain for several years as they mature. They then stop feeding, change color, and swim back up their home river to spawn before, exhausted, they die.

PARENTAL CARE

For many animals, reproduction is a matter of laying eggs and leaving them to hatch. But some animals, notably birds and mammals, show parental care by looking after their young. Parental care makes it more likely that an animal will survive the dangerous early days of life.

▲ DOMESTIC CAT
Many young mammals, including cats, are born helpless—often blind and unable to move much. They are totally dependent on their mother for warmth, protection, and food in the form of milk, which they suckle from her nipples.

▲ ELEPHANT
Some mammals, including elephants and hoofed mammals, give birth to young that can walk and run soon after birth. A young elephant is nurtured by its mother and her female relatives within the herd, who devote many years to its care.

◀ KANGAROO
Young marsupial mammals, such as kangaroos, are born tiny and underdeveloped. They migrate to their mother's pouch and remain there for months, protected and feeding on milk, as they grow and develop.

▲ SCORPION
After giving birth to live young, a female scorpion carries them on her back until they can fend for themselves. Some other arachnids, including certain types of spiders, guard their eggs, even wrapping them in a ball of silk and hauling them around.

Ground-nesting birds hatch from eggs in a well-developed state and are soon moving around. They still receive parental care, however. They usually follow their parent, and sometimes, as in the case of swans, are carried on a parent's back.

▲ BLUE TIT
The young of tree-nesting birds, such as blue tits, hatch blind, naked, and helpless. Both parents spend all day finding insects to feed their offsprings' wide-open beaks so the brood grows and develops rapidly.

GOLDEN STINK BUG ▶
While bees and other social insects look after the young in their colony, most insects just lay eggs and leave them to hatch. However, the golden stink bug guards her eggs and stands over the young hatchlings to protect them from predators.

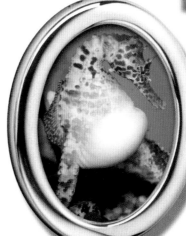

◀SEAHORSE
Around a quarter of fish species show parental care, often by the male. Female seahorses, for example, lay their eggs in a brood pouch on the front of the male's body, where they are incubated until they hatch.

▲ ALLIGATOR
Aside from the few lizards and snakes that guard their eggs, alligators and their relatives are the only reptiles to show parental care. Having laid her eggs, a female guards the nest until they hatch. She then protects her young until they are old enough to be independent.

▼ COLLARED POISON FROG
Some frogs lay a small number of eggs and guard them until, and sometimes after, hatching. The male collared poison frog stays with the eggs until they hatch, then carries the tadpoles to a nearby stream to complete their development.

PENGUIN COLONY

In the cold Antarctic, emperor penguins spend part of their lives on land and part in the ocean. These hardy birds do not exist in isolation, however, but live together in colonies.

Lifestyles

HABITATS

Most animals have a particular set of surroundings, called their habitat, in which they thrive and survive. Each habitat, be it a desert or a tropical forest, is shaped by a number of features including rainfall, altitude (height above sea level), temperature, and what kind of plants grow there. Here is a selection of the many habitats found on Earth, just some of the many habitats found on Earth, with examples of the animals that live in them.

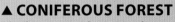

CORAL REEF ▶
Found in shallow, tropical seas, coral reefs are constructed by tiny animals. They provide food and shelter for a rich variety of small fish and other creatures, including predators such as octopuses and sharks.

▲ CONIFEROUS FOREST
Blanketing northern North America, Europe, and Asia, these dense forests of pines and other conifers tolerate long, cold winters. In the short summer they are alive with animals, including insects, seed-eating birds, hares, moose, wolves, and lynx. To survive in winter, many animals migrate or hibernate.

◀ AFRICAN SAVANNA
This vast grassland, dotted with trees, is rich in animal life. It is hot, with alternating rainy and dry seasons. Large herds of grazing animals, such as zebras, are stalked by predators including lions and hyenas.

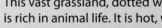

MOUNTAIN ▶
Mountainous regions have several habitats. The higher the altitude, the colder and windier the conditions, and the fewer animals that can survive there. These grazing guanaco in the Andes live between lower forested areas and craggy mountain peaks.

▲ DESERT

In this dry, harsh habitat, temperatures soar during the day and plummet at night. Yet animals do survive there. Many, such as these meerkats, dig burrows for protection from heat, cold, and predators.

TROPICAL FOREST ▶

These dense forests grow in warm, wet areas near the equator and are home to more than half of all animal species. Each level of the forest provides shelter or food for birds, monkeys, and other animals.

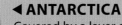

◀ ANTARCTICA

Covered by a layer of ice, lacking in vegetation, and cold all year round, especially during the dark winter, the continent of Antarctica has few permanent animal residents. However, the seas around the continent are rich in animal life including seals, whales, and penguins, some of which breed on Antarctica itself.

DECIDUOUS FOREST ▶

These forests grow where there are warm summers and cool winters, during which the trees lose their leaves. They support many insects that provide food for birds. Other forest animals include squirrels, foxes, bears, and owls, and deer that graze in forest clearings.

HOMES

Although many animals are constantly on the move, others construct homes to provide shelter from the weather and protection from predators for themselves and their young. Some homes, such as a mole's tunnels, last longer than temporary structures, such as birds' nests. On a larger scale, many animals hold and defend a territory in order to protect access to food and water.

❶

Chimpanzee lies back in its leafy nest

❶ OVERNIGHT STAY
After a day's foraging for food in the forest, chimpanzees make simple nests up in the trees where they sleep during the night. They build their nests by folding branches to make a platform that they line with leafy twigs. The next morning the chimps move on, rarely returning to old nests.

❸ TUNNEL AND TRAPDOOR
Trapdoor spiders dig a vertical burrow, closed at the surface by a hinged silk lid camouflaged by twigs and soil. The spider waits in its tunnel home until it feels vibrations produced by passing prey, then darts through the trapdoor to grab its next meal.

❷

A beaver's lodge is built from branches, sticks, and mud

❷ WATER LODGE
Beavers are nature's engineers. These water-loving rodents use their sharp incisor teeth to cut down trees and branches in order to dam streams and create a pond. In the pond they build a lodge—a family home with an underwater entrance. Here beavers feed, breed, and bring up their young, secure from predators.

❸

❹

Trapdoor flies open as spider emerges from tunnel home

❺

❻

A mole eats an earthworm that has fallen into its tunnel

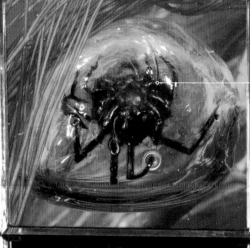

Water spider breathes the air inside its bubble

❹ MOBILE HOME

Some animals carry their homes around with them as extra protection from predators. The hermit crab, which has a soft, vulnerable abdomen, borrows a home by occupying an empty mollusk shell. If danger threatens, it simply withdraws into the shell. When it grows too large for its borrowed shell it moves into a new, larger one.

❺ UNDERGROUND HOME

With cylindrical bodies, short fur, spadelike front feet, and excellent senses of smell and touch, moles are perfectly adapted for building a network of tunnels around a nest or nests. They regularly patrol their tunnels to make repairs and to collect any juicy insects or worms.

❻ AIR BUBBLE HOME

The water spider is the only spider to have a permanent watery home. It spins a web underwater, fills the web with air, and waits in the resulting air bubble, darting out to grab passing prey. The spider goes to the surface occasionally to collect tiny air bubbles on its hairy body to replenish supplies inside the bubble.

These temporary homes, built by birds during the breeding season, come in many shapes and sizes. Nests provide a place where eggs can be incubated and kept warm, as well as shelter for young birds. Great crested grebes build their nests on water, denying access to land-dwelling predators.

❽ TERRITORY

Some animals claim and defend a large home area called a territory. They do this in order to protect their food, water, and mates from rivals. This male cheetah is marking the boundaries of its territory by spraying a jet of strong-smelling urine on a tree.

❾ TREE HOLE

Whether a tree hole is natural or has been excavated, it may provide a home for many species, including woodpeckers and squirrels. A female mountain bluebird builds a nest and lays her eggs in a tree hole, while the male guards her.

❿ PLANT HOME FOR ANTS

Azteca ants are among several species of ants that have a special relationship with plants—in their case, Cecropia trees. The biting ants defend their trees by driving off plant-eating insects and cutting away strangling vines. The tree provides food for the ants, and they nest in hollows within its soft tissues.

Grebe's nest floats on the water

Male mountain bluebird emerges from a tree-hole nest

Azteca ants tend their eggs inside opened tree nest

101

IN THE DARK

Many animal species are not active in daylight, preferring to feed under the cover of darkness. Some are nocturnal, becoming active at night in order to avoid high daytime temperatures, predators, or competition with other species. Others live in habitats, such as the deep ocean, burrows, or caves, where darkness is permanent. All have their own ways of navigating and finding food without the benefit of light.

Fringed wing feathers help to produce silent flight

BARN OWL ▼
This nocturnal hunter is remarkable because it can hunt in pitch darkness. It uses its acute sense of hearing to locate prey, then swoops down soundlessly and grabs its victim with razor sharp talons. Like other owls, the barn owl has big eyes, ideally suited for vision in dim light.

EUROPEAN MOLE ▼
Life underground means that sight and hearing are not important to these champion burrowers. Instead, their heads have a very sensitive, mobile snout with whiskers linked to touch receptors. Using smell and touch, the mole locates its food: earthworms, slugs, and insect larvae that fall into its tunnels.

BLACK-TAILED JACKRABBIT ▶
Like many desert animals, the black-tailed jackrabbit shelters in the shade during the intense daytime heat, emerging in the cool of the night to feed. The jackrabbit uses its long ears to listen for predators, such as coyotes.

TREE WETA ▶
These large relatives of crickets are found only in New Zealand. By day, tree wetas shelter in tree holes, originally excavated by beetles. At night they emerge to feed on plants and small insects. Wetas navigate and sense prey in the dark using their long antennae.

VIPERFISH ▲

The viperfish lives deep in the ocean where no light penetrates. Like many other deep-sea fish, the viperfish has light-producing organs, or photophores. One at the tip of the dorsal fin flashes to lure prey toward the gaping jaws and long teeth. Photophores along the body are used to communicate with other viperfish.

FIREFLY ▶

Also called lightning bugs, fireflies are nocturnal flying beetles that have light-producing organs in their abdomens. These organs contain a substance called luciferin that uses chemical energy to release light. As very little energy is wasted producing heat, it is a highly efficient process. Fireflies use light signals to attract potential mates.

◀ LONG-EARED BAT

Many bats prey on insects. Bats have poor vision, instead using echolocation to navigate and hunt. In flight, the bat releases pulses of high-pitched sounds that bounce off objects. Returning echoes picked up by the bat's ears create a "sound picture," enabling it to pinpoint its prey.

RED FOX ▶

This opportunistic, nocturnal hunter has excellent senses of hearing, smell, and vision. Foxes use their ears to listen for rodents rustling in grass. Their eyes, like those of many nocturnal mammals, have a reflective layer that improves night vision and produces the green glow seen here.

LESSER BUSH BABY ▶

Galagos or bush babies are active at night, jumping between branches in African forests. Their huge eyes allow them to see in near darkness. Large, movable ears enable them to track flying insects so accurately that they can snatch them from the air with their grasping fingers.

TEXAS BLIND SALAMANDER ▶

Animals that spend their entire lives in caves, such as the Texas blind salamander, have no need of sight. This pool-dwelling salamander's eyes are reduced to two tiny black dots. An active predator, it uses touch to locate shrimps and other invertebrates.

ECOSYSTEMS

Within an ecosystem, animals, plants, and other organisms interact with each other and their surroundings. Tropical rain forests are the world's richest ecosystems. Found around the equator, they are hot, wet, and packed with plants that provide food for herbivores, which in turn are eaten by carnivores. A South American rain-forest ecosystem, with a few of its animals, is described here.

1 Fruit bat flies from tree to tree, eating ripe, sweet fruit.

2 Julia butterfly feeds on nectar from flowers.

3 Harpy eagle soars over the canopy, swooping on monkeys, snakes, and other prey.

4 Toucan uses its long, brightly colored beak to reach fruit.

5 Howler monkey eats leaves and lives in a group. Their cries can be heard over long distances.

6 Tamandua is an anteater, which uses its long, sticky tongue to snare ants and termites.

7 Scarlet macaw uses its curved beak to break open fruit or nuts.

8 Blue morpho butterfly feeds on the juices of overripe fruits.

9 Kinkajou is a mammal that grips branches with its prehensile (grasping) tail.

10 Hermit hummingbird feeds on nectar from understory flowers.

11 Tree frog thrives in these humid surroundings, where it eats insects.

12 Green iguana eats leaves and fruits.

13 Eyelash viper is a poisonous snake that preys on frogs, lizards, and small birds.

14 Brazilian tapir uses its mobile snout to feed on grasses, leaves, shoots, and small branches.

15 Wandering spider is agressive, highly venomous, and hunts insects, small lizards, and mice.

16 Hercules beetle roams the forest floor in search of decaying fruit.

17 Giant centipede eats a wide range of prey including insects, lizards, and small birds.

18 Agouti is a rodent that eats fallen fruit and leaves as well as roots.

19 Jaguar is a large predator that stalks and ambushes prey, including tapirs and deer.

Howler monkey's gripping tail helps it cling to branches in its treetop home

◄ EMERGENT LAYER

The tallest trees, which can reach up to 200 ft (60 m) or more in height, protrude above the rest of the rain forest to form the emergent layer. Here the treetops are in full sunlight, but are also sometimes exposed to strong winds and torrential rain. The emergent layer is home to monkeys, bats, butterflies, and birds of prey.

◄ CANOPY LAYER

This is where most animals and the greatest variety of species are found. The canopy consists of a dense "roof" formed by the leaves and branches of tall trees, 50–130 ft (15–40 m) above the forest floor. Food is so abundant here that few animals need to venture to the forest floor. Animals that live here include monkeys, birds, lizards, and tree frogs, but also incredible numbers of insects, many yet to be identified and named.

◄ UNDERSTORY

Little light penetrates this layer, which extends downward from the canopy to the forest floor. Its many shade-loving shrubs and small trees often have large leaves to capture scarce light. Birds, snakes, lizards, and insects are among the animals found here. Some predators, including jaguars, climb into the understory from the forest floor.

◄ FOREST FLOOR

It is dark, hot, and humid here, and there are few ground-covering plants. Ants, beetles, and a multitude of other small creatures feed on leaves, fruits, and dead animals that have fallen from the canopy, releasing nutrients that are recycled for tree growth. Animals that feed on these recyclers are, in turn, hunted by larger predators.

Wingspan of the harpy eagle can reach 6 ft (2 m)

Killer whale

Southern right whale

Mouth opens wide to filter vast amounts of krill from the sea

Crabeater seal

Leopard seal

Flippers allow penguin to swim rapidly and gracefully in pursuit of marine prey

Penguin

Fish

Krill

Phytoplankton

FOOD WEBS

The icy, nutrient-rich oceans around Antarctica abound with life. Plantlike microorganisms use the Sun's energy to produce food that is consumed by shrimplike krill, which are, in turn, eaten by huge whales. This is one of many food chains that together form a food web connecting all the species in the ecosystem. Any ecosystem, whether a coral reef, woodland, or desert, has its own food web.

◄ HOW A FOOD WEB WORKS

A food web shows at a glance what eats what in an ecosystem. In each of the food chains that make up the web, arrows show the direction in which energy flows when one organism consumes another. At each step in a chain, energy is lost. Therefore, less energy is passed on to build and run an animal in the next level.

➊ PRODUCERS

All food webs start with producers—living things that use sunlight energy to make food by a process called photosynthesis. In the case of this Antarctic food web, the producers are microscopic phytoplankton—plantlike organisms that float in the well-lit surface waters. Producers provide the energy that supports all the other species in the food web.

➋ PRIMARY CONSUMERS

Unlike producers, primary consumers cannot make their own food. Instead, they survive by eating the producers, in this case the phytoplankton. Antarctic primary consumers include zooplankton (masses of tiny animals) and krill.

➌ SECONDARY CONSUMERS

Crabeater seals, despite their name, feed almost exclusively on krill that they filter from the water using their unusually shaped teeth. Along with penguins, ice-tolerant fish, and squid they are secondary consumers—animals that feed on primary consumers. However, the categories in a food web are only for guidance: consumers often belong to more than one food chain, and occupy different levels in each.

➍ TERTIARY CONSUMERS

In each food chain, an animal that is eaten passes on only around 10 percent of the energy it received from the animals it ate. The rest is used for movement and maintaining its body or it is lost as heat. Each level, therefore, supports fewer individuals than the one before. At tertiary consumer level these are the elephant seals.

➎ TOP PREDATORS

Leopard seals and killer whales (orcas) are the top predators and consumers in this Antarctic food chain. They are the equivalent of lions in the African savanna, hunting a wide range of prey. They have no natural predators—although orcas will eat leopard seals—so this marks the upper limit of the food web.

➍ Elephant seal

➌ Squid

➋ Zooplankton

Copepods are small crustaceans that form a key part of the zooplankton

TIME OUT

Animals thrive when adequate food, water, and warmth are available. But an animal's environment can change dramatically with the seasons, or even between day and night, especially in cooler, temperate parts of the world. To survive less favorable conditions, such as extreme cold or lack of food or water, some animals use resting strategies, including hibernation, torpor, or estivation. By being less active they conserve valuable energy.

❶ SUSPENDED ANIMATION

Tardigrades or water bears are microscopic creatures that normally live in water. If their surroundings dry out, they curl up and shut down their body systems. They can stay in this state of suspended animation for more than 25 years, but come back to life once water returns.

Tardigrade

Hummingbird

Wings beat so fast that the bird must spend all day searching for energy-rich nectar

American black bear

Desert toad

❷ ESTIVATION

The summer equivalent of hibernation, estivation is practiced by some animals in hot countries. Land snails, for example, seal themselves up to avoid the summer heat and cling together in a state of inactivity. Desert toads survive underground, emerging above ground to lay their eggs only when the rains come.

❸ WINTER SLEEP

In the fall, many bears enter a state of rest called torpor—during which their heart- and breathing rates drop considerably—to avoid cold weather and food shortages. They prepare for torpor by eating greedily to build up fat reserves. Torpid bears sleep in dens, such as hollow trees or caves, but are easily awakened.

❹ REPTILE REST

Reptiles, such as the North American red-sided garter snake, that live in places with cold winters take a winter rest called brumation. Garter snakes gather together in a sheltered location and become sluggish as the temperature falls. In spring, they emerge together to enjoy the warmth.

Mountain-living marmot's size means it must hibernate in a burrow during winter

Marmot

6
Cabbage white butterfly

5

European hedgehog

7
Daubenton's bat

Red-sided garter snake

7 DAILY TORPOR

Some smaller animals, such as hummingbirds and bats, take time out on a daily basis. Hummingbirds keep their body temperature constant during the day. At night, when they rest, their body temperature falls, allowing them to save energy. Bats follow the same strategy except that they show torpor during the day and warm up at night when hunting for insects.

6 DIAPAUSE

Insects, such as butterflies, go through various stages—egg to larva to pupa to adult—during their development. Stages can be delayed to give the insect the best chance of survival. This is called diapause. If a cabbage white butterfly lays eggs in late summer, development stops at the pupa stage over winter and starts up again in the spring.

Chipmunk eats large amounts of food before hibernating, storing some in its winter burrow

Chipmunk

5 HIBERNATION

Mammals are endothermic (warm-blooded) and they need to eat regularly to maintain their body temperature. In winter, small mammals such as marmots, hedgehogs, chipmunks, and bats find this difficult because there is little food and they lose heat easily. To survive, they find shelter and go into hibernation, during which their body temperature and heart- and breathing rates fall dramatically.

Hard shell protects snail as it estivates

Giant land snails

ARCTIC

NORTH
AMERICA

1 RED CROSSBILL

Found in the northern forests of North America and Europe, red crossbills eat conifer seeds. In years when seeds are in short supply, a mass movement, or irruption, occurs as crossbills fly south in search of food.

2 GRAY WHALE

Each spring and fall, gray whales migrate between summer feeding grounds in the Arctic and winter lagoons off Baja California, Mexico, where the females give birth.

3 SPINY LOBSTER

Adult Caribbean spiny lobsters live in coral reefs but in the fall they migrate to deeper waters to avoid colder conditions. Unusually, they travel together and in single file until they reach open water.

4 EUROPEAN EEL

After starting life in the western Atlantic Ocean, young eels migrate east to European rivers, a journey that can take three years. After many years there they migrate back to their birthplace to breed.

5 GREEN TURTLE

Every three years or so, these marine reptiles take a break from feeding on seagrasses off the coast of Brazil and make the 2,500-mile (4,000-km) round trip to Ascension Island in the south Atlantic to mate and breed.

SOUTH
AMERICA

MIGRATION

While many animals never leave their habitats, others regularly migrate (move from one habitat to another) in order to avoid excessive heat or cold, to find food, or to breed. The journeys can be short, like those of the European toad, but sometimes the distances covered are immense. Migration often coincides with the changing seasons, but for some, such as the eel, it spans a lifetime.

ASIA

EUROPE

7 ALPINE IBEX
Strong jumpers and surefooted climbers, these agile mountain goats live at high altitudes in summer but move to lower areas during the cold winter months when food is scarce.

10 EUROPEAN TOAD
As adults, European toads spend most of their time on land. But every year, when they emerge from their winter hibernation, they follow the same route back to the ponds where they hatched in order to breed.

8 COMMON SWIFT
These superb fliers spend the winter in Africa, feeding on insects that they catch on the wing. In April they fly north to Europe to breed during the summer, before returning to Africa in the fall.

AFRICA

9 BLUE WILDEBEEST
In the biggest mammal migration on Earth some 1.5 million wildebeest, a type of antelope, follow a triangular route across the African savanna in search of water and fresh grazing. On the way, many wildebeest fall prey to cheetahs, hyenas, crocodiles, and other predators.

AUSTRALIA

11 BOGONG MOTH
Common in southern Australia, bogong moths escape the intense summer heat by flying by the millions to the Australian Alps. Here they roost in crevices and caves. In the cooler fall, they migrate to inland pastures to lay their eggs.

6 ARCTIC TERN
This seabird migrates an incredible 25,000 miles (40,000 km) each year. Arctic terns breed in the Arctic during the long summer days. As fall approaches, they make the epic journey to the Antarctic, where the southern summer is just beginning.

ANTARCTIC

111

LIFE IN THE EXTREME

Wherever there is warmth, water, and plenty of food, animals will prosper. The same is not true of baking, dry deserts, the dark depths of the oceans, or the icy-cold Arctic and Antarctic, where the harsh conditions would kill most animals. However, some hardy animals can survive in these places. They are adapted to life in the extreme by, for example, having no need to drink water, being resistant to the enormous pressure in the deep ocean, or by being well insulated against biting cold.

ANTARCTIC ICEFISH ▶

In addition to having "antifreeze" proteins to stop it from freezing, the Antarctic icefish also has thin, transparent blood that circulates easily in the cold.

COLD WATER ▶

Because fish are ectothermic (cold-blooded), the temperature of their insides matches that of their surroundings. So, in icy Arctic waters fish should freeze to death. Yet Arctic fish such as the arctic cod survive the cold. They have "antifreeze" proteins that prevent ice crystals from forming so their blood and other body fluids stay liquid.

Polar cod

▼ UNDER PRESSURE

Deep in the ocean, animals must tolerate pressures that would crush a human. Sperm whales, which survive dives to depths of 10,000 ft (3,000 m), have a flexible rib cage that allows their lungs to collapse. In the dark ocean depths, deep-sea fish such as the gulper eel produce light to lure prey, and have large mouths to grab it.

Gulper eel

Eelpout

White crab

Sperm whale

Tubeworm

HYDROTHERMAL VENT ▲

In the deep ocean, hydrothermal vents are openings through which vent hot, mineral-rich water erupts. Bacteria that can tolerate the harsh water and use it to make sugars that feed tubeworms and crabs. In turn, these animals are energy from the chemicals in vent water and eaten by predators such as eelpouts.

Arctic fox

Emperor penguins

Wood frog

COLD ON LAND ▲
The arctic fox's thick coat and insulating body fat enable it to withstand temperatures as low as -40°F (-40°C). Similar conditions are tolerated in the Antarctic by male emperor penguins as they huddle together, incubating eggs. During bitterly cold Canadian winters, wood frogs freeze solid then thaw out the following spring.

Desert jerboa

Camel

DESERT HEAT ▶
Some animals thrive in the scorching heat. The desert jerboa does not drink, shelters from the daytime heat in a burrow, and emerges at night to feed on seeds from which it gets the moisture and can go without water for weeks, then when water is available, make up the loss in minutes. Camels tolerate high temperatures of waterless deserts.

DESERT PUPFISH ▲
Found in the desert springs of southwest North America, this small fish is very tolerant of harsh conditions. It can survive in water that is six times saltier than the sea and as hot as ˉ13°F (45°C).

PARTNERSHIPS

Day-to-day survival is a tough proposition for most animals. Some improve their chances by forging partnerships with other creatures. Symbiosis, the term that describes all such relationships, comes in various forms, including mutualism and commensalism. Mutualism is a partnership that benefits both partners. Commensal relationships, like that of the pearlfish and sea cucumber, have only one beneficiary.

Ant protects aphids from enemies

Buffalo tolerates oxpecker's presence

Oxpecker eats irritating parasites

Aphid sucks sap from plants

▲ OXPECKER AND BUFFALO

Oxpeckers are birds that live in the African savanna and have a close relationship with buffalo, rhino, and other big mammals. Perching on their partner, they dig out ticks and other irritating parasites. The oxpecker gets food, while its partner gets relief.

ANTS AND APHIDS ▲

Some aphids and ants have a mutually beneficial relationship. Aphids are insects that suck sugar-rich sap from plant stems. Excess sap, called honeydew, oozes from their rear ends and is harvested by ants to drink. In turn, ants protect aphids from predators, such as ladybugs.

Anemone's tentacles

Clownfish among tentacles

◀ CLOWNFISH AND SEA ANEMONE

Most animals that stray into the stinging tentacles of sea anemones are paralyzed and then eaten. Not so the clownfish, which appears to be immune. It lives close to the anemone, retreating between the tentacles should danger threaten. In turn, it may lure prey for its host to eat.

◄ PEARLFISH AND SEA CUCUMBER

The eel-like pearlfish spends its days protected inside the sea cucumber. At nightfall, it exits through its host's anus to feed. In the morning, it waits for the anus to open, then swims back in.

Pearlfish emerges from sea cucumber's anus

Sea cucumber lives on the seabed

CLEANER SHRIMP AND MORAY EEL ▼

This cleaner shrimp should be a tasty snack for a moray eel, or any of its other "client" fish. Yet the shrimp remains unharmed as it removes irritating parasites from the predator's skin, earning itself a meal.

Cleaner shrimp removes parasites

Pseudoscorpion uses pincers to latch on

▲ PSEUDOSCORPION AND INSECT

Tiny, clawed arachnids, pseudoscorpions employ a unique means of transportation to find new places to feed. They use their pincers to hang on to a handy fly, beetle, wasp, or other big insect, as they are flown to a new location. Only the pseudoscorpion benefits, but their host is not harmed.

Moray eel remains still

Dugong is not hurt by the remora

Remora attaches to host

REMORA AND PARTNER ▶

Commensalism is well illustrated by tropical remora fish. They use a suckerlike pad on top of their heads to attach to sharks, turtles, or marine mammals called dugongs. The remora gets free transportation, while its partner neither gains nor loses anything.

115

Thin paper wall made from chewed wood

Worker returns from foraging with food

COLONIES

Across the animal kingdom there are many examples of animals living together in social groups or colonies. The closest knit and most organized colonies are found in the group of insects that includes ants, bees, and wasps. Individuals within these insect societies belong to specific castes or classes, each with their own tasks, such as food gathering or rearing young. A wasp colony like this one is dominated by its queen.

❶ WASP CASTES

For most of its life the nest contains only two castes, the larger queen and her smaller workers. The queen lays eggs and controls the colony. Her workers have various tasks, including building and repairing the nest, foraging for food and feeding larvae, and defending the nest from intruders. In late summer larger larvae develop into males and new queens, which fly from the nest and mate. The males soon die, but the young queens seek shelter and hibernate. The old colony dies and its nest is now empty.

❸ NEST

A wasps' nest is cut away here to show its structure. In spring, a solitary queen starts to build the nest, mixing chewed wood fibers with saliva to make a papery substance. When the first workers hatch, they continue the process of building the central comb of cells which will house more eggs. As spring turns to summer the multistory nest, built from the top downward, is completed.

❷ QUEEN WASP

When a young queen emerges in the spring from hibernation, last fall's mating means she is ready to lay fertilized eggs. First, she finds a nest site and constructs a small comb of paper cells in which she lays her eggs. When they hatch, the sterile female workers continue the work of building the nest while their queen lays more eggs. The queen releases chemicals called pheromones to prevent her workers from becoming queens, and to control their behavior so they perform their various tasks.

❹ CELLS

These hexagonal (six-sided) chambers are remarkable examples of animal architecture. Although, like the rest of the nest, they are made of paper, their shape makes them enormously strong. The hexagonal shape also means that a lot of cells can be packed into the small space inside the nest. For the queen and her workers, knowing how to build the nest and its cells is instinctive.

❺ LARVAE

In each cell the queen lays one egg that hatches into a larva or grub. The larva grows rapidly as it is fed on a diet of chewed-up caterpillars and other insects brought to the nest by workers. When it is fully grown the larva spins a silken cap to close its cell, and becomes a pupa. After a few days, a worker wasp emerges from the cell, ready to take on its duties.

117

PARASITES

In parasitic partnerships one animal, a parasite, exploits the other, the host, in order to obtain food, shelter, or to reproduce. Endoparasites, such as flukes and tapeworms, live inside their hosts, while ectoparasites, such as lice, ticks, and mites, live outside. Other types of parasite include parasitoid wasps and brood parasites, like cuckoos.

HEADLICE ▶

Seen here magnified and in false color, headlice are wingless insects that live on human hair. They grip the hair shafts with their front legs to stop them from being dislodged by combing or washing. When they descend on to the scalp, they use their mouthparts to pierce skin and suck blood, causing itching in the human host.

▲ CUCKOO

The female common cuckoo is a brood parasite that tricks another bird into raising her offspring. She lays one egg in the host bird's nest. After hatching, the young cuckoo pushes the host's eggs out of the nest. Now the center of attention, it grows rapidly.

◀ PARASITOID

A parasitoid is an animal, typically a wasp, that lays its eggs on or in a living host. The host provides food for larvae when they hatch, and dies in the process. Here wasp larvae are emerging from a dead caterpillar.

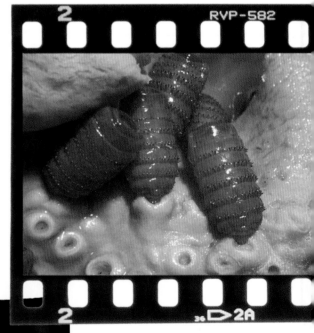

◀ LAMPREY ▶

This jawless fish is an ectoparasite of trout, salmon, and other fish. It uses its suckerlike mouth and rows of small, pointed teeth to clamp onto the side of its host. The lamprey's rasping tongue wears a hole through the skin, then sucks out blood and tissues.

▲ BOTFLY LARVAE

The botfly lays its eggs on the skin of mammals. The eggs hatch into larvae that burrow under the skin and grow until they resemble large maggots (above). They then push their way back to the surface and fall to the ground to form a pupa that will develop into an adult fly.

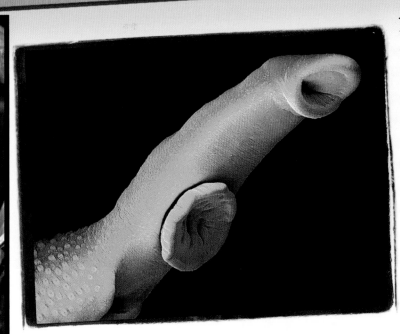

◄ SCHISTOSOME FLUKE

This highly specialized flatworm lives in the blood vessels that surround the human bladder or intestines. Male and female worms live together, held in place by the male's suckers (left). Together, they produce millions of eggs that may pass out of the body to infect new hosts.

ISOPOD ►

Some members of this group of crustaceans are ectoparasites of fish. They attach to and erode the skin around the eyes, mouth, or gills of their host, and feed on blood and tissues. Isopod parasites make the fish less streamlined so it swims less efficiently. Other isopods are not truly parasitic and feed on discarded food scraps.

▲TICK ON FROG

This blood feeder pierces the skin of its host, in this case a frog, using its hooked mouthparts. These hold the tick firmly in place for hours or days as it fills up with blood, swelling greatly as it does so. Fully engorged, the tick falls off its host and digests its meal.

TAPEWORM ►

Hooks and suckers anchor the scolex (head) of this tapeworm to the intestine of its host, in this case a cat. The ribbonlike flatworm can grow to more than 33 ft (10 m) in length. It has no mouth, but absorbs food from the host's intestine through its surface.

◄ MITES

Like ticks, mites are relatives of spiders. Some are free-living, but many are parasites of both invertebrates and vertebrates. This mass of parasitic mites carried on the back of a beetle is sucking out its tissues.

ALIEN SPECIES

Animals that live together in a particular habitat have evolved in ways that ensure an overall balance of numbers. However, if alien species are introduced accidentally or deliberately to a habitat, that balance can be destroyed. If the invasive species has no natural predators and a good supply of food, it will multiply uncontrollably and may cause native species to disappear. The five examples below are among the world's worst invasive alien species.

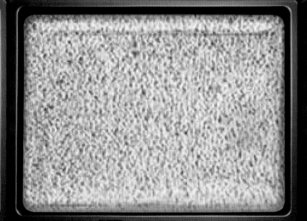

▲ STOAT
This small but ferocious predator was imported into New Zealand in the late 1880s to control rabbits, another introduced species. But these active hunters also eat eggs and chicks and have had a devastating effect on native bird species, most notably the kiwi.

▲ CHINESE MITTEN CRAB
Named for its furry claws, this native of China arrived in Europe and the US on ships. It lives in fresh water and breeds at an incredible rate. Mitten crabs will eat nearly anything—disrupting communities of native animals—and cause erosion by digging burrows in riverbanks.

▲ CANE TOAD

This large South American toad was introduced to Australia in 1935 as a pest controller. Their skin produces predator-killing poisons, making them hazardous to inquisitive family pets. Since they eat everything, from snakes and frogs to mammals, they have caused the decline of many native species.

▲ RABBIT

Rabbits were introduced to Australia in 1859. Only 24 were released but they multiplied so rapidly that soon there were millions. Rabbits outcompete native plant-eaters for food, making some extinct. By removing ground cover they allow soil to blow away and cause serious erosion. They are difficult to control, even with fences.

▲ ROSY WOLF SNAIL

This predatory snail was introduced to Tahiti and nearby islands in the 1970s to control another introduced species, the giant African land snail. But instead of targeting its intended prey, the rosy wolf snail attacked native snail species. Most of the native snails are now extinct and those that remain are endangered.

NEW VARIETIES

In the natural world, species change over time in a process called evolution. Evolution works through natural selection, with animals best adapted to a particular habitat more likely to survive long enough to breed and pass on their features to new generations than those that are less well adapted. For thousands of years, humans have used artificial selection (selective breeding) to produce new varieties of domesticated (tamed) animals for their own use. Genetic modification is the latest form of human interference.

African wildcat

Pet cat

Breeding has produced a flattened face

Aurochs

Gray wolf

▲ CATS
When agriculture developed in the Middle East and Egypt more than 8,000 years ago, harvested crops had to be stored. These stores were devastated by rodents such as rats and mice. Farmers domesticated wild cats to kill the rodents. Later, selective breeding produced the varieties of cat breeds seen today.

Chihuahua

Domesticated cockerel

Junglefowl

▲ DOGS
From Great Danes to Chihuahuas, all breeds of dogs are descended from wolves. Wolves were the first animals to be domesticated, about 13,000 years ago. Initially they were used for hunting, but, later, selective breeding was used to produce a variety of working dogs and pets.

▲ CHICKENS
The junglefowl found today in the forests of southeast Asia is the bird from which domestic chickens originated about 8,000 years ago. People tamed these birds to obtain both eggs and meat as food, then bred them to create new varieties.

Hereford bull

◄ CATTLE

Various types of wild cattle, including European aurochs, were first domesticated 10,000 years ago. Cattle are used for milk, meat, and leather. More recent selective breeding has produced some breeds that excel at milk production, and others that are primarily farmed for meat.

Wild boar

▼ GLOWING MICE

Genetic modification involves taking specific genes (instructions for a particular characteristic) from one organism and introducing them into another. For example, a jellyfish gene introduced into mice makes them glow. Scientists hope these genetic-engineering techniques will aid research into human diseases.

Young farm pigs

Mice glow green under blue or ultraviolet light

▲ PIGS

Over thousands of years, pigs have been domesticated in different places around the world at least seven times, probably because wild boar are very adaptable and are easy to look after. Selective breeding has produced animals that are less hairy and less aggressive than their wild boar ancestors. Domestic pigs are used mainly for meat, but some dwarf breeds are popular as pets.

Glossary

abdomen
The part of an animal's body that contains reproductive and digestive organs. It forms the rear part of the body of insects, crustaceans, and arachnids.

amphibian
An ectothermic (cold-blooded) vertebrate, such as a frog or newt, that lives partly in water and partly on land.

annelid
A type of worm, such as an earthworm, with a soft, rounded body that is made up of segments.

Antarctica
The continent around the South Pole that is covered by ice sheets.

antenna (plural: antennae)
A long sensory structure, or feeler, on the head of insects, crustaceans, and some other arthropods.

arachnid
An arthropod with four pairs of legs, such as a spider or scorpion.

Arctic
The region around the North Pole, and a word that describes animals that live there.

artery
A blood vessel that carries oxygen-rich blood from the heart to an animal's tissues.

arthropod
An invertebrate, such as an insect, crustacean, or arachnid, that has a hard body case and jointed legs.

bacteria
A group of simple, single-celled organisms, the most abundant on Earth.

bird
An endothermic (warm-blooded) vertebrate, such as an eagle, that has a beak, feathers, wings, and can fly.

calcium carbonate
A white, solid mineral salt that forms or reinforces the shells of mollusks and the cuticle of crustaceans.

camouflage
The way in which an animal uses its shape and/or color to blend in with its surroundings.

carapace
The hard shield that covers and protects the head and thorax of crustaceans such as lobsters and crabs.

carbon dioxide
A waste gas released by an animal as a result of cell respiration (energy release).

carnivore
Specifically, a member of an order of mammals, including cats and wolves, that eats mainly meat. Also, any animal that is a meat-eater.

cartilage
A tough, flexible tissue that makes up the skeleton of cartilaginous fish, such as sharks, and forms part of the skeletons of other vertebrates.

cell
One of the many tiny living units that together make up an animal's body. Other living things, such as bacteria and plants, are constructed from one or many cells.

cephalopod
A type of mollusk, such as an octopus, that has a distinct head with large eyes and tentacles with suckers.

cephalothorax
The front section of the body of spiders and other arachnids to which four pairs of legs are attached.

chordate
A member of a group of animals that includes vertebrates, such as fish and reptiles.

compound eye
A type of eye, found in insects and crustaceans, that is made up of many small units.

crustacean
An arthropod, such as a crab or shrimp, that has two pairs of antennae and several pairs of jointed legs.

cuticle
The hard, protective outer layer (exoskeleton) of arthropods such as insects and crustaceans.

echinoderm
A marine invertebrate, such as a starfish or sea urchin, with an internal skeleton and a body divided into five equal parts.

echolocation
The use of reflected sounds, employed by bats and dolphins, to locate objects, especially food.

ecosystem
A community of interacting living organisms and their environment, such as a tropical forest or a coral reef.

ectothermic
Describes an animal, such as a frog or snake, whose internal temperature varies with that of its surroundings.

endothermic
Describes an animal, such as a duck or a rabbit, whose internal temperature remains the same regardless of the external temperature.

energy
The capacity to perform work, required for all life functions including growth and movement.

equator
An imaginary line drawn around the Earth halfway between the North and South poles, which divides it into northern and southern hemispheres.

enzyme
A substance that speeds up chemical reactions—including the break down of food molecules during digestion—inside animals and other living organisms.

evolution
The process by which species change over many generations, thereby giving rise to new species.

exoskeleton
The hard outer covering of animals such as insects and crustaceans.

extinction
The permanent disappearance of a particular species of animal or other living organism.

fish
A general name used to describe several groups of vertebrates, including sharks and bony fish, that live in water and have streamlined bodies with fins.

food chain
A pathway that links together selected species within a habitat to show what eats what.

gene
One of the instructions, stored inside cells, required to build and operate an animal's body, and which is passed on from parents to offspring.

gill
A structure, found in fish and other aquatic animals, used for taking in oxygen and releasing carbon dioxide under water.

gonad
An organ, such as the testis or ovary, that produces sex cells used in reproduction.

habitat
The natural home of a species of animal or other living organism.

herbivore
An animal, such as a cow, that eats only plants.

hibernation
A state of deep sleep used by some smaller mammals to survive cold winters when food is scarce.

insect
An arthropod, such as a beetle or butterfly, with three pairs of legs, usually two pairs of wings, and a body divided into three parts.

insectivore
An animal, such as an anteater, that feeds on insects. Also a member of an order of mammals that includes moles and hedgehogs.

invertebrate
An animal, such as an earthworm or insect, that does not have a backbone.

krill
A shrimplike crustacean that forms the main food source of baleen whales.

larva (plural: larvae)
A young animal, such as a caterpillar, that undergoes metamorphosis to become an adult, such as a butterfly.

lung
A structure, found in mammals and air-breathing animals, used for taking in oxygen and releasing carbon dioxide.

mammal
An endothermic (warm-blooded) vertebrate, such as a lion or bat, that has hair or fur and feeds its young on milk.

metamorphosis
A major change that happens to the body of certain animals, including amphibians and many insects, as they mature into adults.

microorganism
A living thing that can only be seen under a microscope.

migration
A journey undertaken by an animal, often on a seasonal basis, from one habitat to another in order to find food and/or breed.

mollusk
A soft-bodied invertebrate, such as a snail, mussel, or squid, that is typically protected by a hard shell.

mucus
A thick, slippery fluid secreted by animals for lubrication and protection.

muscle
An animal tissue that can contract (get shorter) in order to pull and create movement.

natural selection
The process whereby organisms that are better adapted to their surroundings survive longer and produce more offspring. It is the driving force of evolution.

nectar
A sugary liquid produced by flowers to attract animals, such as butterflies, that pollinate them.

nerve
A bundle of long, specialized cells that rapidly relay signals from one part of an animal's body to another.

nocturnal
Describes an animal that is active at night, but inactive by day.

northern hemisphere
The half of the Earth that is north of the equator.

nutrient
A substance taken in by an animal in its food that is needed for normal functioning.

nymph
A stage in the life cycle of certain insects. Nymphs look like smaller, wingless versions of adult insects.

omnivore
An animal, such as a black bear, that eats both plant and animal foods.

organ
A structure, such as the heart or an eye, that is made of two or more types of tissues and plays a specific role in keeping an animal alive.

organism
An individual living thing, such as an animal or a plant.

oxygen
A gas taken in by an animal that is used up during cell respiration (energy release).

parasite
An organism that lives inside or on the body of another species, and exists at the expense of its host.

pheromone
A chemical "message" released by an animal that has an effect on other members of its species.

photosynthesis
The process by which plants and plantlike plankton use sunlight energy to combine carbon dioxide and water to make food.

plankton
A term describing the mass of tiny animals (zooplankton) and plantlike protists (phytoplankton) that float in both the sea and fresh water.

pollinator
An animal such as a butterfly that, while visiting flowers to feed, transfers pollen from one flower to the next, enabling them to reproduce.

predator
An animal, such as a lion, that kills and eats other animals.

prey
An animal that is killed and eaten by another animal, the predator.

producer
An organism, such as a plant, that makes its own food using sunlight energy, and provides nutrients and energy for the animals that eat it.

protein
One of a group of substances made by an animal's cells that are essential for life and that include enzymes and the structural proteins found in hair and spiders' silk.

pupa (plural: pupae)
The resting stage in the life cycle of many insects, including beetles and wasps, during which they change from a larva to an adult with a complete change, or metamorphosis, in body shape.

reptile
An ectothermic (cold-blooded) vertebrate, such as a crocodile or snake, that has a waterproof, scaly skin and lays eggs on land.

savanna
A grassland habitat with widely spaced trees found in hotter regions of the world, notably in parts of Africa.

species
A group of organisms consisting of similar individuals that can breed together.

sterile
Describes an animal, such as a worker bee, that is unable to reproduce.

symbiosis
A close relationship between members of two different species that may be mutually beneficial or one-sided.

system
A set of linked organs inside an animal's body that perform a specific function or functions.

tadpole
The larva, or immature stage, of amphibians.

territory
An area claimed and defended by an animal in order to protect sources or food or water, to mate, or to bring up young.

thorax
The central body region of an insect, which is combined with the head in arachnids and crustaceans. An alternative name for the chest of a vertebrate animal.

ungulate
A mammal, such as a horse or pig, that has toes tipped with a hard hoof.

vein
A blood vessel that carries oxygen-poor blood from the tissues toward an animal's heart.

venom
A poisonous substance released by an animal (a venomous animal), such as a rattlesnake, in its bite or sting in order to immobilize or kill prey or enemies.

vertebrate
An animal, such as a fish, amphibian, reptile, bird, or mammal, that has a backbone.

Index

Acknowledgments

DK would like to thank:
Charlotte Webb for proofreading; Jackie Brind for the index; Steven Carton for editorial assistance; Richard Ferguson for the ecosystems pop-up; KJA-artists.com for illustration; staff at the Zoology Library of the Natural History Museum, London, for access to the collection there; and Robert J. Lang for the origami animals.

The publisher would like to thank the following for their kind permission to reproduce their photographs:

Key:
a–above; b–below/bottom; c–center; f–far; l–left; r–right; t–top

6-7 NHPA / Photoshot: Martin Harvey (c). **8** Science Photo Library: Steve Gschmeissner (clb); P. Hawtin, University of Southampton (cra); Dr Kari Lounatmaa (tr); Astrid & Hanns-Frieder Michler (cl). **9** Science Photo Library: Sinclair Stammers (c). **10** Corbis: Jose Luis Palaez, Inc (ca/earthworms). DK Images: Frank Greenaway / courtesy of the Natural History Museum (tr); Colin Keats / courtesy of the Natural History Museum (bl); Harry Taylor / courtesy of the Natural History Museum (cla/sea fan). FLPA: imagebroker / J. W. Alker (c/bearded fireworm); Roger Tidman (fbr/tick). Getty Images: Stephen Frink (fclb). Science Photo Library: Dr, George Gornacz (c/marine flatworm); Nature's Images (bc/land planarian); Matthew Oldfield (ftl/giant barrel sponge); Dr. Morley Read (tc/velvet worm). **11** Corbis: Tom Brakefield (br/breaching whale). DK Images: Jerry Young (crb/crocodile). Getty Images: Karl Ammann (fcr). Science Photo Library: Matthew Oldfield, Scubazoo (ca/mantis shrimp). SeaPics.com: Doug Perrine (cl/Nautilus); Mark Strickland (clb/Cone shell). **13** FLPA: Paul Hobson / Holt (bl) (cb); Derek Middleton (cra) (tr). **16-17** The Natural History Museum, London: McAlpine Zoological Atlas / Z, 11, Q, M, / plate XVIII (cr). **20** Corbis: Peter Johnson (c). **20-21** Getty Images: Foodcollection (bc). Photolibrary: Ross Armstrong (ca). **21** NHPA / Photoshot: Jason Stone (tc). **22** FLPA: Minden Pictures (cr/giant tortoise). Still Pictures: Biosphoto / Heuclin Daniel (cl). **23** Alamy Images: Tim Gainey (cl). Corbis: Momatiuk-Eastcott (c/albatross). DK Images: Barrie Watts (br); Jerry Young (tl/Crocodile). FLPA: Fritz Polking (cr). Getty Images: Ken Lucas (cb). **26** Alamy Images: Arco Images GmbH (fbl); William Leaman (cr). Corbis: Bettmann (ca/Trogons). **26-27** Alamy Images: Arco Images GmbH (tc) (br). 27 Alamy Images: Arco Images GmbH (tr) (fcrb). Ardea: Rolf Kopfle (fbr). **28** Corbis: Visuals Unlimited (cb/Komodo dragon). DK Images: Jerry Young (cra/crocodile). Getty Images: Stockbyte (cb/sunlounger). **29** Corbis: Michael & Patricia Fogden (clb/thorny devil). DK Images: Jan Van Der Voort (bc/worm lizard) (cb/gila monster); Jerry Young (fcra/puff adder). 30 NHPA / Photoshot: Stephen Dalton (tr/flying frog). Science Photo Library: Paul Zahl (tc). **30-31** Getty Images: John Burcham / National Geographic (c). **31** FLPA: S & D Maslowski (tc); Chris Mattison (cl/Couch's spadefoot) (c/Darwin's frog); Minden Pictures (fcr/glass frog); Minden Pictures / Piotr Naskrecki (cl/Caecilian). Photolibrary: Emanuele Biggi (fcl/lungless salamander). **32** NHPA / Photoshot: A.N.T. Photo Library (clb/lamprey). **32-33** Corbis: Amos Nachoum (c/barracuda school). **33** Alamy Images: Stephen Fink Collection (crb/moray eel). FLPA: Michael Durham / Minden Pictures (tc/white sturgeon). Photolibrary: Paulo De Oliveira (cla/hatchetfish). **34-35** Photolibrary: Ed Robinson (c). **35** Corbis: Lawson Wood (bl). SeaPics.com: Marc Chamberlain (tr). **36** Science Photo Library: Matthew Oldfield, Scubazoo (tr). **37** Alamy Images: David Adamson (tr). iStockphoto.com: edfuentesg (br/water background). **38** Science Photo Library: David T. Thomas (tr). **39** FLPA: Nigel Cattlin / Hilt Studios (fbr/large tick); Roger Tidman (fbr/small tick). Getty Images: Photographer's Choice (cr/plug hole). **40** Corbis: Martin Harvey (clb/ant with leaf). **41** DK Images: Harry Taylor / courtesy of the Natural History Museum (tl/striped shield bug). **42** SeaPics.com: Doug Perrine (cla). **42-43** Alamy Images: imagebroker (c). Science Photo Library: Dr. Keith Wheeler (bc/limpets). **43** SeaPics.com: Marc Chamberlain (cla); Mark Strickland (cra) (ca); Jez Tryner (cr); James D. Watt (br). **44** FLPA: D. P. Wilson (cl). Science Photo Library: Nature's Images (br); Dr. Morley Read (bl). **45** Corbis: Jose Luis Palaez, Inc (cl). FLPA: imagebroker / J. W. Alker (br); D. P. Wilson (cr). Science Photo Library: Dr, George Gornacz (tr). **46** Corbis: Lawson Wood (bc). DK Images: Geoff Brightling / Peter Minister - modelmaker (tr/box jellyfish); David Peart (tc). Adam Laverty: (tl). SeaPics.com: Doug Perrine (fbl); Richard Hermann (cla). **47** Corbis: Stephen Frink (c/diver & background). Getty Images: Brandon Cole (bl). SeaPics.com: Brenna Hernandez / Shedd Aqua (br). **48** The Natural History Museum, London: John Sibbick (tl). **49** Alamy Images: Natural History Museum (c). **50** Ardea: Tom & Pat Leeson (cl). Auscape: Francois Gohier (bc). NHPA / Photoshot: Joe Blossom (tr). Ignacio De la Riva: (cr). **51** Bruce Behnke: (cra). FLPA: Minden Pictures (bl). Paul H. Humann: (cl). naturepl.com: Paul Johnson (tl). **52-53** naturepl.com: Anup Shah (c). **54** SeaPics.com: Steve Drogin (c). **55** SeaPics.com: Michael S. Nolan (c). **56** Corbis: Mary Ann McDonald (tl). FLPA: Minden Pictures (fcl/giant anteater). Photolibrary: Nick Gordon (cra/Vampire bat); Stan Osolinski (bc). **57** Corbis: Galen Rowell (cr/Muntjac). **58** Alamy Images: blickwinkel (tl). NHPA / Photoshot: Anthony Bannister (cb). Photolibrary: Marian Bacon (c); Michael Fogden (bc). **58-59** Alamy Images: Steve Allen Travel Photography (c). FLPA: Richard Dirscheri (cb). NHPA / Photoshot: Stephen Dalton (tc). **59** FLPA: imagebroker / Stefan Huwiler (tc). naturepl.com: Anup Shah (cb). NHPA / Photoshot: Stephen Dalton (c). Photolibrary: David B. Fleetham (bc). **62** Ardea: M. Watson (cr). FLPA: Minden Pictures (c); Sunset (cl). Photolibrary: Eyecandy Images (bl/mirror); Per-Gunnar Ostby (br). Science Photo Library: Claude Nuridsany & Marie Perennou (bl). **63** FLPA: Minden / Frits Van Daalen / FN (cr). naturepl.com: John Waters (br). Photolibrary: Richard Packwood (cl). **66** Ardea: Paul Van Gaalen (c); Andrey Zvoznikov (cla). Corbis: Visuals Unlimited (clb). naturepl.com: Alan James (cl). **66-67** Alamy Images: David Crausby (c/sunglasses). FLPA: imagebroker / Marko K´nig (c). **67** Alamy Images: Juniors Bildarchiv (clb). Ardea: John Cancalosi (cla); Ron & Valerie Taylor (crb). Corbis: Martin Harvey (cra). Science Photo Library: Ken Read (cr); Peter Scoones (tr). **68** Alamy Images: Nadia Isakova (br). Science Photo Library: David Aubrey (tl). **69** Alamy Images: Rick & Nora Bowers (bl); Redmond Durrell (tl). **70** Alamy Images: Arco Images GmbH (bc). FLPA: Minden Pictures (c). Photolibrary: Tobias Bernhard (cr). **70-71** Alamy Images: tbkmedia.de (tc). Elizabeth Whiting & Associates: Lu Jeffery (c). **70-72** naturepl.com: Lynn M. Stone (bc). 71 Alamy Images: The National Trust Photolibrary (c). FLPA: Minden Pictures (tc). naturepl.com: Jane Burton (bc). Photoshot: Woodfall Wild Images / Richard Kuzminski (bl/Turkey vulture). SeaPics.com: Mark Conlin (cl). 72 Alamy Images: blickwinkel (cr) (cl); Phil Degginger (bl). **73** Alamy Images: D. Hurst (cr/iphone); Peter Arnold, Inc. (crb); Stuart Simmonds (cl); WildPictures (clb). Ardea: Premaphotos (bl). **74** Corbis: Reuters / Handout (br). DK Images: Colin Keats / courtesy of the Natural History Museum (crb) (bc/rolled pill woodlice); Jerry Young (bc). **75** Alamy Images: Kevin Ebi (cl/Snow geese); Roger McGouey (br). DK Images: Frank Greenaway / courtesy of the Natural History Museum (ca). Barry Gooch: South Carolina Dept. of Natural Resources (bc/octopus). Photolibrary: Waina Cheng (crb/blue-tailed skink). 76 naturepl.com: John Cancalosi (c/Chameleon); David Kjaer (cb); Constantinos Petrinos (ca); Michael Pitts (cr); Premaphotos (bc); T. J. Rich (bl); Markus Varesvuo (clb). **76-77** SeaPics.com: Mike Veitch (c). **77** Corbis: Tom Brakefield (bl/Okapi). naturepl.com: E. A. Kuttapan (tl); Doug Allan (cr); Ingo Arndt (c/caterpillar); Philippe Clement (ca); Mike Wilkes (fclb/moth). **78** Alamy Images: Premaphotos (br). 79 Alamy Images: Neil Hardwick (cr); Rolf Nussbaumer (ca). Science Photo Library: Nature's Images (bl). 80 Alamy Images: Images of Africa Photobank (c); Stock Connection Blue (cl). **80-81** Getty Images: Stephen Krasemann (cb/bighorn rams). 81 Alamy Images: Jason Gallier (clb/European robin) (cl); David Osborn (cr). **82** Alamy Images: Stephen Fink Collection (cb). **83** Alamy Images: AfriPics.com (cla); Fabrice Bettex (cr); Daniel Demptser Photography (br); WildPictures (cl). SeaPics.com: Kevin Schafer (tc). **84** Corbis: Tom Brakefield (bl). Still Pictures: Tom Vezo (bl). **84-85** Alamy Images: Kirsty Pargeter (c). **85** FLPA: Hugh Lansdown (cl); Sunset (br). **86** Alamy Images: blickwinkel (br); Daniel Valla FRPS (ca/Magnificent frigate bird). DK Images: Frank Greenaway / courtesy of the Natural History Museum (tc/Female birdwing butterfly); Colin Keats / courtesy of the Natural History Museum (tr/male birdwing butterfly). FLPA: David Hosking (ca/Red frigate bird). NHPA / Photoshot: Nick Garbutt (cr/female proboscis monkey); Martin Harvey (c/male probascis monkey). **86-87** Alamy Images: Larry Lilac (c). **87** Alamy Images: Holger Ehlers (cl); Zach Holmes (bc). DK Images: Peter Cross / courtesy of Richmond Park (ca/Male red deer). iStockphoto.com: BlackJack3D (br). **88** Corbis: Frank Lukasseck (bl). Mike Read: (cl). **88-89** Alamy Images: PictureNet Corporation (c/fans). FLPA: Robin Reijnen (tc). naturepl.com: Roger Powell (c/Lyrebird). NHPA / Photoshot: John Shaw (bc). **89** Corbis: Vince Streano (bc). FLPA: Michael Gore (cr). National Geographic Stock: Tim Laman (c). naturepl.com: Shattil & Rozinski (tc). **90** DK Images: Frank Greenaway / courtesy of the Natural History Museum (tc). FLPA: Nigel Cattlin (ca); Mike Jones (c). **90-91** Getty Images: Image Source (c/egg carton). **91** Ardea: Steve Hopkin (cb/Butterfly eggs). DK Images: Harry Taylor / courtesy of the Natural History Museum (c/Guillemot egg). **92** Alamy Images: M. Brodie (br/mature eagle); David Gowans (tl/newly hatched chick) (crb/parent with offspring). Corbis: W. Perry Conway (cr/eagle chick). Getty Images: Martin Diebel / fstop (cl/curtain section of booth); Siri Stafford (cr/curtains). **92-93** Getty Images: Yo / Stock4B Creative (cr/green section of boothe). **93** FLPA: Chris Mattison (cla/adult frog) (cra/wings expanding) (fcla/frog shrinking tail) (fcra/adult dragonfly) (tl/frog with tail); Minden / Rene Krekels / FN (ftr/emerging adult dragonfly); Minden Pictures (ftl/tadpoles). Getty Images: Siri Stafford (tl) (br) (c) (tr). naturepl.com: Hans Christophe Kappel (cb/adult butterfly). NHPA / Photoshot: George Bernard (tl/nymph). SeaPics.com: Daniel W. Gotshall (fbr/mature salmon); Chris Huss (br/young salmon); Jeff Mondragon (crb/egg). Still Pictures: Wildlife / A. Mertiny (fcrb/hatchling). **94** Ardea: Ferrero-Labat (cla). **95** Ardea: Tom & Pat Leeson (cl); Pat Morris (crb); Tom Watson (tl). César Luis Barrio Amorós: Fundacion AndigenA (bc). Corbis: Frank Lane Picture Agency / Philip Perry (tr). Photolibrary: Ken Preston-Mafham (cr). **96-97** naturepl.com: Tom Vezo (c). 98 Alamy Images: Reinhard Dirscherl (ca). Corbis: Theo Allofs (br). FLPA: Mark Newman (tr); Ariadne Van Zandbergen (bl). **98-99** Ardea: G. Robertson (bc). **99** Alamy Images: James Clarke Images (tc/keys). Corbis: Martin Harvey (tl); Minden Pictures / Mark Raycroft (br). FLPA: Minden Pictures (tr). **100** Ardea: Densey Clyne (cb); John Daniels (bl); Don Hadden (crb). Corbis: Rose Hartman (ca). FLPA: Minden Pictures (tc). Photolibrary: Harry Fox (br). **101** Ardea: Masahiro Iijima (cb). FLPA: imagebroker / Michael Krabs (ca); Minden Pictures (br) (bl). **102** DK Images: David Peart (tr); Rollin Verlinde (bl). FLPA: Minden Pictures (br/Jackrabbit). 102-103 Corbis: Mark Dye / Star Ledger (c). **103** Photolibrary: David M. Dennis (br); David Haring / Dupc (crb); Wallace Kirkland (cra). SeaPics.com: Gregory Ochocki (tl). **108** Photolibrary: Andoni Canela (fcl/Palm tree). Science Photo Library: Steve Gschmeissner (cla). **109** Ardea: Francois Gohier (cl). Photolibrary: Andoni Canela (fcr/Palm tree). **112** Alamy Images: tbkmedia.de (tl). Corbis: Denis Scott (fbl) (cb/tubeworm). DeepSeaPhotography.Com: (cr) (cb). National Geographic Stock: Paul Nicklen (tc); Norbert Wu / Minden Pictures (bl/Gulper eel). Science Photo Library: Dr. Ken MacDonald (br). **112-113** Getty Images: Per-Eric Berglund (c). **113** Alamy Images: Arco Images GmbH (tl); Elvele Images Ltd (tc); Don Hadden (c); Image Source Black (br). NHPA / Photoshot: T. Kitchin & V. Hurst (tr). Still Pictures: A. Hartl (bl); Wildlife / O.Diez (cl). **114** Alamy Images: Elvele Images Ltd (cla); Antje Schulte (tl). DK Images: David Peart (bl). **114-115** Science Photo Library: Georgette Douwma (tc). **115** Alamy Images: cbimages (clb). Photolibrary: Oxford Scientific (tr). SeaPics.com: Doug Perrine (br). **116** DK Images: Jerry Young (br). **118** FLPA: Nigel Cattlin (clb); Tony Hamblin (tl). Photolibrary: Carol Geake (crb). Science Photo Library: Rondi & Tani Church (bc); Steve Gschmeissner (cla). **119** Alamy Images: blickwinkel (bl). Corbis: Kevin Schafer (tr/ticks on frog). Science Photo Library: Eye of Science (br); Andew J. Martinez (cl); David Scharf (tl) (cr/Crab with fish). **120** Alamy Images: Arco Images GmbH (cra) (tr); Gavin Thorn (bc); Wildlife GmbH (c). Photo Biopix.dk: Niels Sloth (br). **120-121** Alamy Images: J. R. Bale (c) (cr/Rosy wolfsnail on fern). **121** Alamy Images: Photo Resource Hawaii (cra) (br) (tr); Jack Picone (tl) (cl); A & J Visage (tc). Ardea: Kathie Atkinson (bl). Corbis: John Carnemolla (cb). FLPA: Minden Pictures (c/fence). NHPA / Photoshot: Daniel Heuclin (cla). **122** Ardea: Kenneth W. Fink (bc). The Natural History Museum, London: Michael Long (cla). **122-123** Alamy Images: Oote Boe (c)

All other images © Dorling Kindersley

For further information see:
www.dkimages.com